NEW FORMS

PLANS AND DETAILS FOR CONTEMPORARY ARCHITECTS

EDITED AND DESIGNED BY **THE PLAN**

CONTENTS

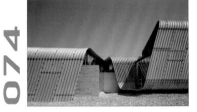

FOREWORD

I have always considered the job of the architect to be one of the most difficult and complex. It is creative yet technical, requires interpersonal skills yet is always constrained by economic considerations, statutory regulations and the physical laws of what is technically possible. In short, the architect is a demiurge.

New Forms aims to provide architects with a useful tool, starting with the very first, perhaps most crucial instant of any new project – the creative moment. It is based on the concept that while architectural projects clearly require a certain location and a client brief indicating specifications and budget, they also involve the very personal resolve of an architect to follow up on an initial creative spark. That inspirational, intellectual moment – consisting of aspects such as forms, colours, materials and transparencies – needs this resolve to carry it through the successive phases to realization.

In this book, a series of architectural projects are presented where innovative form has particular significance. Presentation is by order of size, starting with detached family homes through to large public complexes such as university buildings and concert halls. Geographically the book spans the world, from Europe to the Americas and Japan. The organic forms of Ben van Berkel's Villa NM and Fernando Romero's Ixtapa House contrast with the sharp geometries of Eduardo Souto de Moura's two houses, the Macallen Residential Complex by Office dA and Erick van Egeraat's Metzo College. The discreet curves of Reichel Architekten's Wellenhaus or Norman Foster's Chesa Futura are flanked by the stark linear solidity of projects like the Documentation and Information Centre by Engel und Zimmermann. Likewise, the deliberate attempt to de-structure volume in buildings like the Summer

House by Enrique Browne or the private house by Gri e Zucchi is set alongside projects where uncompromising forms and regularly repeated geometries emphasize mass, as in Simmons Hall by Steven Holl and the Richard E. Lindner Athletics Center by Bernard Tschumi. There are projects like the Galway-Mayo Institute of Technology by Murray O'Laoire where an essentially simple composition is denoted by complex sail-shaped volumes overlooking the sea, or the Shipping and Transport College by Neutelings & Riedijk where the interplay of façades and volume geometries point to new creative developments in architecture.

Also examined is the exceptional research of architect Shuhei Endo whose sheet steel roof on the Springtecture B house takes the theme of folding shapes to the extreme. This is followed by a look at how the alternation of materials can be used as a means of composing and de-composing volume, as in the Cube Tower by Carme Pinós or Thom Mayne's Campus Recreation Center. Finally, *New Forms* looks at architectures that stand as icons of new design trends. Toyo Ito's Meiso no Mori Municipal Funeral Hall and Rem Koolhaas' Casa da Música are two examples, prototypes of future developments whose importance goes beyond their individual identity.

This book is intended as the first of a collection that will look at conceptual yet practical aspects of architecture today: colour, material, transparency, energy saving, corporate identity, landscape, and icons. The aim of this thematic approach is to uncover the primary element around which a particular project grows. Closely related, these concepts become even more significant when assorted into yin-yang pairs. The geometrical material force of this book, for example, dialogues

with the impalpable chromatic identity of colour. Transparency and material can be seen as project oxymorons. Energy saving, geared to optimizing energy and mechanical efficiency, juxtaposes but also runs parallel to corporate identity, which seeks expression through brand-enhancing architecture. Finally the landscape and icons pair contrasts the effort to blend into the environment with the drive to create a landmark: introspection and purity vying with showmanship and assertion.

New Forms is a compendium of twenty of the most important avant-garde projects of the past decade. Whether by celebrity architects or budding talents, they all strive for quality, innovation and originality, helping us understand where contemporary architecture is going, what new codes are being developed and the forms that creativity is taking at an international level. This edition would not have been possible without the backing of the architectural journal *The Plan*.

First published in 2001, this international publication was designed from the start to be a review with a difference. Since then, it has kept faith with its original goal over and above changes along a natural growth curve. *The Plan* narrates architecture not just through pictures and accompanying text but also by giving readers an in-depth insight into each building's technical features. Architecture is not just seen from the outside; considerable space is given to examining the technology that makes it possible. During *The Plan's* first years, a great deal of effort went into developing a highly legible code of interpretation. Technical drawings and their captions, photographs, text and graphic design were all finely tuned to provide interesting, informative reading. As a result, we have created something that did not exist before: the successful combination of an architecture lifestyle journal and a technical manual. *The Plan* is not just a coffee table magazine with stunning views of what's new in architecture. It is a design and construction reference work for practitioners. We have given *New Forms* the same hallmark features as the journal. An overview of contemporary and avant-garde architecture, it provides a constant dialogue between image and construction detail, adding a completeness that only a book can achieve. Designed with the practitioner in mind, the book will be inspirational throughout the design and building process, from that initial creative moment through the successive phases of problem-solving and construction.

Throughout the production process, the expertise and vast experience of Thames & Hudson were invaluable. Benefitting from the knowledge and creativity of this longstanding publishing house has been a priceless learning experience for all of us on *The Plan* team. My grateful thanks go especially to Guglielmo Bozzi Boni whose outstanding professional and personal qualities were crucial to the success of this project.

Nicola Leonardi
Editor in Chief, *The Plan*

SHAPES TO AN END

Architecture is all about place. Exploring an unfamiliar city, we search for landmarks by which to orientate ourselves and to define the character of the place we are in. From the twin spires of Cologne Cathedral, to the dome of St Peter's and the flared skeleton of the Eiffel Tower, height gives them visibility and shape confers identity. Both qualities are needed to stand out in the concrete jungle. Few visitors to New York gazed in rapture at the Twin Towers, even though they were the tallest; the popular favourites have long been the Empire State Building with its set backs and phallic crown and the needle spire of the Chrysler Building. The Sydney Opera House is an icon for the city, dominating the waterfront. Labyrinthine Asian cities have traditionally lacked such markers, making them even more baffling to the outsider.

Back in 1919, Bruno Taut wrote of the need for a Stadtkrone – a secular equivalent to the cathedral spire – but few were built outside of Manhattan until the first global wave of high-rise construction began in the 1960s. Most of those towers were the product of commercial expediency and bureaucratic frugality; banal stacks of offices and apartments designed in a debased modern style. Shape was banished along with ornament. Now, the pendulum has swung to the opposite extreme, and the boom cities of Asia and the Middle East are becoming menageries of exotic creations, each vying for attention. Few of these eccentric forms have any logical justification or relationship to their location. The chief culprit is the computer, which has fostered a free-for-all. Software enables a Gehry or a Hadid to realize buildings that have the spontaneity of their sketches, but it also allows unprincipled developers and mediocre architects to create bombastic follies that turn cities into sci-fi movie sets.

The traditional Vitruvian principles of firmness, commodity and delight are as relevant today as when they were proposed, two millennia ago. They apply just as well to exceptional and experimental buildings as to the humbler majority. Talented architects welcome constraints – of cost, size, programmatic needs and site limitations – as a challenge to their invention. Take them away and you enter a realm of fantasy, in which everything is possible but the connection with reality is sundered. The theme of the 2008 Venice Biennale, Architecture Beyond Building, generated a show that many found vacuous, unfocussed and self-indulgent. Invited to crystallize a vision in a couple of months, most of the respondents dusted off an unrealized project, a minor variation on a familiar theme, or scavenged whatever was closest to hand.

Most of the installations, and the talking heads accompanying them, were instantly forgettable. Few of these hasty improvisations contained a fraction of the creativity that their makers put into the projects they hope to realize – and why should we expect otherwise? Architecture is a public and collective art that strives to enrich the world we live in. Utopian visions and structural daring are welcome, but need to serve utilitarian as well as aesthetic and intellectual ends.

The sixteen projects selected for this book are compelling for their originality and thoughtfulness. Form and function, exteriors and interiors are interwoven and dependent on each other. They create or reinforce a sense of place and represent a significant advance in their designers' vocabulary of forms. Half the selections are residential, six are institutional; there is also an office tower and a crematorium.

The house has always been a laboratory for adventurous architects, affording an opportunity to work out ideas of structure, space and

materiality on a small scale with a single supportive client, before applying the lessons learned to larger projects. Like the chair – a form that challenges every designer – the house is a basic building block and a problem that can be solved in an infinite variety of ways. In town and country, as a place to nurture a family or as a solitary retreat, the stand-alone residence demands that an architect become fully engaged in concept and detail.

The Villa NM draws on UN Studio's Mobius House and classic modern villas to create a hybrid that mutates as one moves around and through it, shifting from rectilinear to curved forms, and from one level to another, compressing and enlarging interior space and views of an idyllic site in upstate New York. Norman Foster's Chesa Futura in the mountains above St Moritz adapts the Swiss tradition of wood construction raised above the snow-covered ground, and gives it an entirely fresh form: a bubble of apartments that open up to the sun and shut down to the north. In contrast to these unique works, Springtecture B is another iteration of Shuhei Endo's ongoing investigation of corrugated metal, which can be coiled to enclose public or private space.

The fluid sprayed concrete canopy of Toyo Ito's Meiso no Mori crematorium outside Gifu, Japan, was inspired by floating clouds and distant mountains, and it assumes a form that is as light and elegant as a brushstroke in an ink-wash landscape painting. The apparent simplicity of the undulating roof and gracefully tapered columns belies the complexity of its design, which required several hundred evolutionary cycles of a software program.

Steven Holl's Simmons Hall dormitory for the Massachusetts Institute of Technology and Bernard Tschumi's Lindner Athletics Center for the University of Cincinnati both make brilliant use of confined sites. A porous membrane is how Holl describes the punched-out and cut-away façade of the linear block he inserted onto a narrow strip of land. By articulating the mass as separate blocks he reduces its impact on the street, and he breaks into the grid of uniform square windows with notches expressing the sculptural common rooms that punctuate the cellular structure. Tschumi accepted an even tougher challenge, and the kidney-bean plan and long spans of his diagrid exoskeleton are a response to the jagged site and the underground services that the building had to step over. The taut compression of the exterior contrasts with the five-storey skylit atrium, a vertiginous volume as thrilling as any of the moves on the sports field outside.

The Casa da Música in Porto is an enigmatic composition of folded planes; an angled concrete block that seems to hover above its open urban site. The outline of the principal auditorium is clearly expressed in the profile of the building, and the expansive areas of glazing provide glimpses of lobbies that build anticipation for what is to come. A multilevelled cluster of secondary spaces flows around the main hall, choreographing the movements of its users. It's hard to believe that this competition-winning design, with all its complexities, is an enlarged version of an unrealized house in Rotterdam.

Curvilinear or angular, cantilevered or contained, each of these buildings is pregnant with meaning. Each is shaped by need and programme, and expresses a marriage of inspiration and utility. They lift the spirits of their users, and provide models for architects who reject the notion of form for form's sake.

Michael Webb

FORMS IN ARCHITECTURE

A review of contemporary architectural forms reveals a wide range of projects that together reflect the sedimentation of multiple objectives and methods. Contemporary architecture is a picture gallery of how central ideas underpinning the design process have developed. Modern buildings and the way they fit into the built or natural environment are the result of the manifold requirements made upon the contemporary architectural project. Clients and architects espouse projects with defined functions and aims, which are then translated into tangible physical form. The concepts are myriad, as many as there are ways of social living, for the world's cultural geography is still highly diversified. To be defined as contemporary, form and volume – that special combination of geometry and function – must exhibit experimentation, research and new perspectives. Technological investigation, sustainable solutions in their broadest sense, and experimentation with materials and structures are all prerequisites for inclusion in the contemporary-architecture bracket. It is also a mindset that goes hand in hand with widespread communication of the architectural solutions adopted, which in turn reflects the belief that architecture is an art destined for society, and as such to be judged by society. For contemporary architecture places itself at the hub of modern living, a discipline that changes the environment but that is, by the same token, changed by it.

Being contemporary does not require declarations or manifestos. Concepts are simply translated into tangible form. Yet freedom of interpretation is guided by project rationality that steers choices and decisions. In this way, form and volume, i.e. the final architecture, are an answer to a special mix of problems and requirements that has no readymade solutions.

A stark, fragmented architectural programme making a forthright statement in the landscape may seem the antithesis of more compact geometries that blend into their surrounds. Yet they are both the product of a talent to translate a building's requirements in terms of function and impact on the environment. Although antithetical in the residential modes they propose, the two single family houses by Eduardo Souto de Moura at Ponte de Lima nonetheless demonstrate the same holistic approach to the architectural project. In one case, the aim is to preserve privacy and intimacy, while in the other the programme provides sweeping views over the steeply sloping countryside. The volume of the first house follows the natural incline, while the second projects forcefully over the landscape. Both possess clarity of vision and deftness of design, reflected also in the sleek elegance of the interiors.

The summer house in Zapallar, Chile, opts to dig into the steep slope against which it is built. The three descending volumes, dedicated for either night or day zones, seem to spring from the hillside all the better to cantilever dramatically over the void, fanning out like leaves on a tree.

The Cube Tower in the Mexican city of Guadalajara is characteristically split into three parts, the combination of different materials amplifying this expressive architectural feature. Carme Pinós' building is a landmark not so much for its height as for its distinctive architecture and materials which highlight its unusual shape: a central concrete structural core on either side of which two multiple-storey blocks cantilever out, their inner glazed envelope shielded by a wooden slat construction acting as a brise-soleil. The wooden mesh pattern is repeated endlessly across both outer façades, highlighting the three-component composition. The volume is further broken up by the omission at irregular intervals of

three storeys on both projecting blocks, an architectural feature that allows light to penetrate the building and provides enough natural ventilation to do without artificial air conditioning. It is a good example of contemporary architecture where form and profile respond to project requirements.

An example of architecture that weaves architecture and location-specific materials is Norman Foster's Chesa Futura in St Moritz in Switzerland's Engadine region, famous for its up-market tourist offering. The futuristic façade is clad in finely tapered, natural colour larch shingles, a feature that harks back to ancient building techniques in this mountainous region. The rounded volume combines with the natural wood shades to allow this sizeable building to blend comfortably into the environment.

The compact mass of Erick van Egeraat's Metzo College in the Netherlands is a landmark building, yet one that fits into the slightly undulating landscape dotted with trees. The truncated pyramid shape conceals a well-knit programme of educational spaces in compliance with the trade school requirements of the college. Classrooms flow into community areas, which in turn lead to more confined spaces for small group study. Plant and equipment are contained in the partially superposed storeys that provide selective views onto the outside, while three large vertical structures contain the staircase wells. Volume – and hence form – dictate but, at the same time, are enhanced by the façade system: opaque metal panel cladding and glazing that underscore the parallel and oblique structural elements.

The Villa NM, designed by Ben van Berkel and UN Studio, is an example of geometrical mathematical forms and volumes intricately superimposed as if to form a sort of three-dimensional transmission belt. Wide, concrete-framed glazed walls look out in various directions over the countryside, commanding sweeping views from their elevated position. Similarly, the prism shapes of the Casa da Música in Porto by OMA/Rem Koolhaas confer a monumental character to the building, making it the landmark of its urban setting. Multifaceted façades combine glazed sections that fill with light and depth and opaque sections, creating a volume that seems to be actively expanding into the surrounding plaza. In contrast, the Shipping and Transport College in Rotterdam, designed by Neutelings & Riedijk, follows a rigorously geometrical programme. The two contributions by Bernard Tschumi and Morphosis/Thom Mayne to the University of Cincinnati in Ohio are examples of contrast at close quarters. Tschumi's sports building puts the accent on blending materials and structures to create a dynamic curved outer perimeter that is strictly delineated by a repeated triangular structural grid, visible also from the inside. The nearby Campus Recreation Center by Morphosis/Thom Mayne offers huge, open linear volumes to accommodate sports and recreational and cultural activities. Dramatic cantilevered volumes are gathered into a single sweeping complex by a sinuous undulating roof. The centre becomes a pivotal node for the whole campus. Similar weaving circulation systems are also part of the modular regularity of Steven Holl's Simmons Hall at MIT in Cambridge (MA). Here, volume is part of architectural form by its absence, the external modular grid forming a semi-transparent shield for the voids that lie behind.

Francesco Pagliari

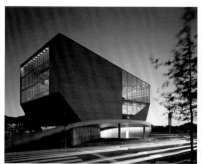

VILLA NM
UPSTATE NEW YORK, USA

UN STUDIO / BEN VAN BERKEL

Ever since the first studio diagram came out, the plans for Villa NM have always reminded me of a Bach Two-Part Invention – the invention being Philip Johnson's Glass House which here unfolds into two separate units like a gesture parting spaces that the American architect had overlooked.

The first plans for Villa NM date from 2000, the year when designs like the Mobius House or the magnetic resonance imaging lab at Utrecht University began to circulate the name of Ben van Berkel as an experimenter in complex geometries. Unlike other projects, I felt this one would never come to fruition – it was so perfect, no doubt it would crumple on contact with everyday reality.

The layout of space, clean and complex, was the stuff of pure thought, not suited to physical materialization. But I have had to eat my words: not only is the villa built, but its geometry even seems to match with invisible features of that first diagram, like the lie of the land and the effective distribution of space inside.

Villa NM is the summer residence of a young couple from New York City. It stands on a gentle slope and takes its cue from the terrain. To van Berkel's mind, it is a platform for "experiencing landscape": 360° glazing commands the surrounding woodlands. The sloping ground is used to generate space and volume layout in this house. A simple cube splits into two distinct bodies: the kitchen drops away with the land, the sleeping area juts up and out to form covered parking for two cars. The real fireworks lie in how these areas merge and meet.

The walls twist up and over to form a new floor; what was floor in turn becomes wall in a surprising reversal of planes. Five surfaces twist propeller-like while another five bend to produce a bifurcation in space.

From the outside, this screw action provides a virtuoso formal display; inside, the unexpected space effect hovers between biomorphism and sci-fi, somehow contriving to divide up the areas without losing visual and structural continuity.

Outwardly the villa blends with its surrounds: walls and floors match the colour of the ground; large glass panes reflect back the scenery. At times it seems to invite comparison with a work by American artist Dan Graham in which glass panes standing out of doors make one lose one's bearings between reality and reflection. Reclining on, almost suspended above, the ground, Villa NM is built nearly all in pre-fab parts. But, unlike a house by Richard Neutra, the parts in cement and iron, which may be clad in wood, have an unexpected flow to them. The innovation here lies in the extreme ductility of surface, employed so as to serve design aims which are mainly structural and not purely aesthetic. This is what van Berkel calls the inclusive principle, one single mould that includes all design requirements: from structural to formal aspects, and from organization of space to details of construction. In keeping with this principle, the furnishings are architect-designed: the kitchen worktop curls on itself and every feature seems to respond to some generating idea.

Part of a long line of American suburban villas, beginning with Mies' Farnsworth House down to Glenn Murcutt's ethereal dwellings, Villa NM seeks to provide a blueprint for home design, architecture taking its cue from our requirements. This project may not be a point of arrival so much as an interesting point of departure towards a galaxy of novel space effects.

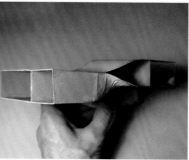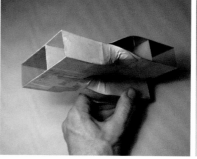

■ First Floor Plan – Scale 1:200

1. Covered parking
2. Entry
3. Toilet
4. Kitchen – dining
5. Living
6. Bedroom
7. Bathroom
8. Landing
9. Bedroom
10. Master bedroom
11. Master bathroom
12. Roof

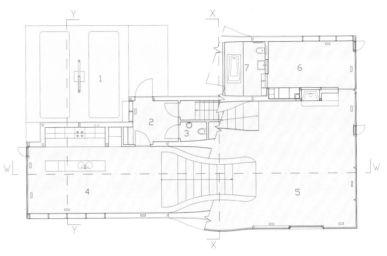

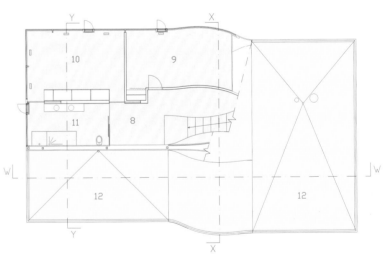

■ Second Floor Plan – Scale 1:200

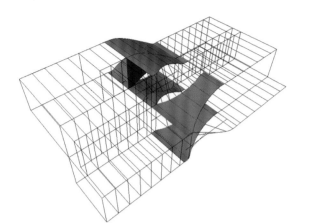

■ Preliminary perspective drawings – curved surfaces

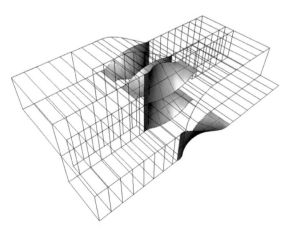

■ Preliminary perspective drawings – twisted surfaces

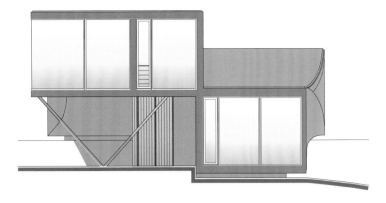

■ North Elevation - Scale 1:150

■ East Elevation - Scale 1:150

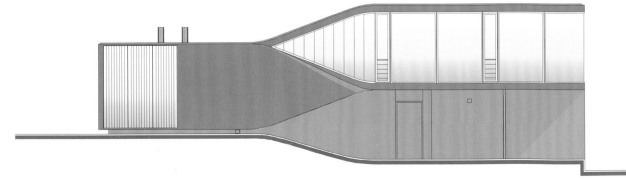

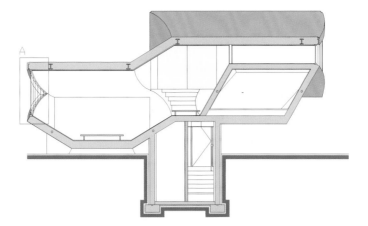

■ XX Cross Section – Scale 1:150

■ YY Cross Section – Scale 1:150

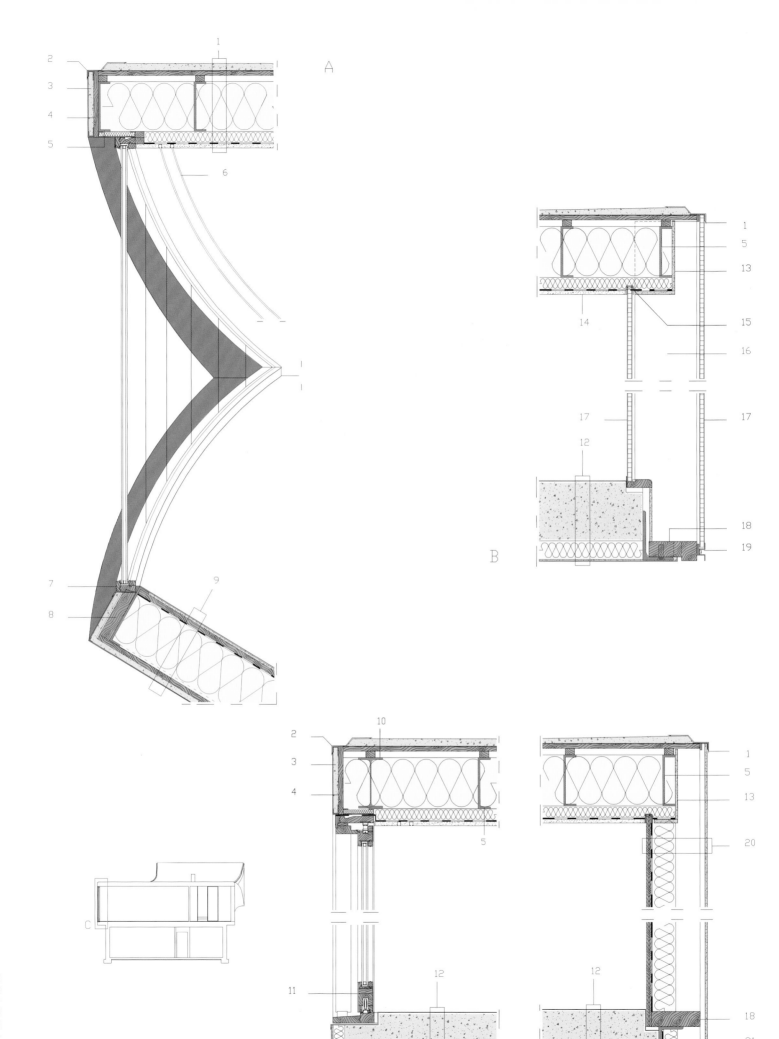

A

B

C

**DETAILS A, B AND C
EXTERNAL WALLS AND GLAZING
VERTICAL SECTIONS – SCALE 1:15**

1. Dark grey elastomeric
waterproofing finish on
gypsum render with metallic
mesh, 3/4" (19 mm) multilayer
wood panel on framework of
1 1/2 x 1" (38 x 25 mm) timber,
7 7/8 + 2" (200 + 50 mm)
fibreglass board insulation,
vapour barrier, ceiling in 5/8"

(15 mm) gypsum board panels
with white elastomeric finish
2. Steel flashing painted dark grey
3. Dark grey elastomeric
waterproofing finish on
1" (25 mm) thick gypsum render
with reinforcing mesh
4. 3/4" (19 mm) thick multilayer
wood panel
5. 10 x 2" (254 x 50 mm) steel
C-profile supporting roof
6. Track for closure system
7. Dark grey wood double

glazing assembly with
1/4 – 1/2 – 1/4" (6 – 12 – 6 mm)
glass, Pilkington Eclipse advantage
laminated glass with bronze-
coloured low-emissivity film
8. 2" (50 mm) thick wood stud
9. 1/8" (4 mm) resin floor painted
white, 1/4" (8 mm) concrete
levelling layer, 3/4" (19 mm)
multilayer wood panel, vapour
barrier, 8 7/8" (225 mm)
fibreglass board insulation,
10 x 2" (254 x 50 mm) steel

C-profile structure, 3/4"
(19 mm) multilayer wood panel
elastomeric waterproofing
finish on 1" (25 mm) thick gypsum
render with reinforcing mesh
10. IPE 200 steel profile
supporting roof
11. Wood sliding door painted
dark grey with 1/4 – 1/2 – 1/4"
(6 –12 – 6 mm) double glazing,
Pilkington Eclipse Advantage
laminated glass with bronze-
coloured low-emissivity film

12. 1/8" (4 mm) resin floor,
9 1/4" (235 mm) reinforced
concrete slab, 3" (75 mm)
fibreglass board insulation,
elastomeric waterproofing
finish on 1" (25 mm)
thick gypsum render
with reinforcing mesh
13. 3/8" (10 mm) thick
fibre cement panel
14. False ceiling in 5/8" (15 mm)

gypsum board panels with
white elastomeric finish
15. Painted 1 1/8 x 1 3/8"
(30 x 35 mm) aluminium
U-profile for fixing cellular
polycarbonate panel
16. 10 x 2 3/8" (254 x 63 mm)
wood frame upright supporting
hollow wall in cellular
polycarbonate panels
17. 3/4" (20 mm) thick cellular

polycarbonate sheet
18. Painted wood fixed to
7 1/2 x 5 1/8" (190 x 130 mm)
steel L-profile
19. Aluminium omega profile below
cellular polycarbonate sheets
20. 3/8" (10 mm) fibre cement
panel with grey elastomeric
waterproofing finish,
4 x 4 x 1/4" (100 x 100 x 5 mm)
vertical steel profile (parallel

to plane of section), 4" (100 mm)
fibreglass board insulation,
vapour barrier, double 3/4"
(20 mm) multilayer wood
panel with white elastomeric
finish on inside face
21. 9 7/8 x 4 7/8" (250 x 125 mm)
steel C-profile supporting wood
elements under insulated wall

IXTAPA HOUSE – ZIHUATANEJO, MEXICO
LCM / FERNANDO ROMERO

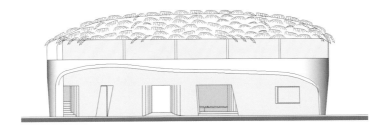

West Elevation – Scale 1:300

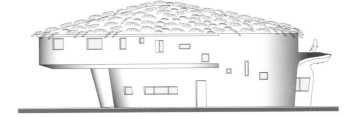

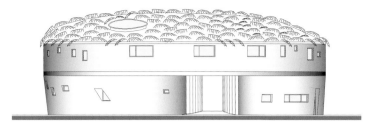

In Nahuatl, the Uto-Aztec language, Ixtapa means "white sand place". The house is sited on a private beach on the Pacific coast in north- eastern Guerrero state, 150 mi (250 km) above Acapulco. Here maximum water depth is 39 – 79 ft (12 – 24 m), ocean currents are moderate and there is a plenty of sea life. The climate is hot and fairly humid; temperatures range from 75°F to 90°F (24°C – 32°C) in summer, dropping to 70°F (21°C) in winter. There are heavy rains in summer (at night) and during part of autumn. The winter is dry with average temperatures around 79°F (26°C). The sun shines almost every day of the year.

Situated as close to the ocean as possible, the building has been designed to meet the different needs of a beach house. Its circular ground plan is typical of many primitive populations throughout the world, a feature that is here highlighted by the use of local building materials.

The architectural project wanted to maintain traditional building features of the area yet at the same time create an innovative building through the use of modern technology. Site orientation was based on the final building plan: the north side of the building is fairly closed while the completely open south, sea-facing side has wide terraces. All around the house, a sweeping garden hosts a large variety of the very diverse vegetation existing at Ixtapa Zihuatanejo. The many tropical flower species characteristically conserve their brilliant green colours, even in the driest periods.

The house has a concrete skeleton that contains plant and services and supports the roof over the living space. It is divided into two parts: on the ground floor facing the terrace in front of the swimming pool are the kitchen, TV room and main bedroom; on the upper floor, more bedrooms and bathrooms. Technical plants are contained in the spaces between the hardcore structure and the outer skin. Stones, natural colours and the "Palapa" roof – a conventional local roofing material of dried palm leaves – are the main construction materials. The project uses a combination of local craft skills and contemporary imported materials that are guaranteed to be resistant to the hot, salt-laden atmosphere.

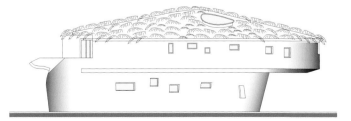

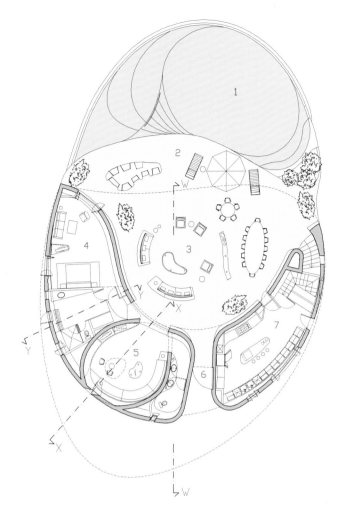

■ Ground Floor Plan – Scale 1:300

1. Swimming pool
2. Terrace
3. Dining room
4. Main bedroom
5. TV room
6. Entrance
7. Kitchen
8. Bedroom

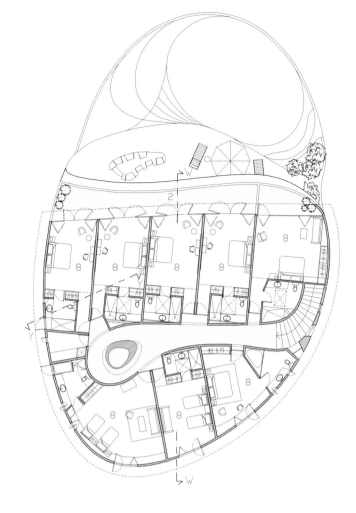

■ First Floor Plan – Scale 1:300

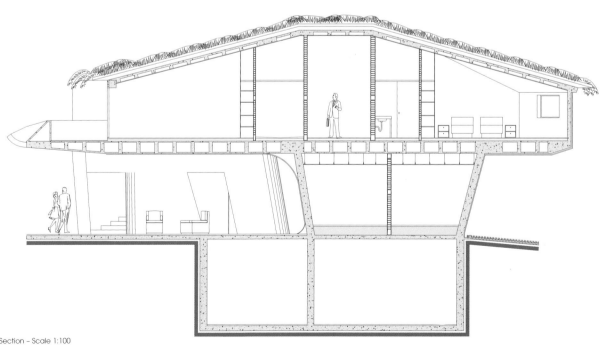

■ WW Section – Scale 1:100

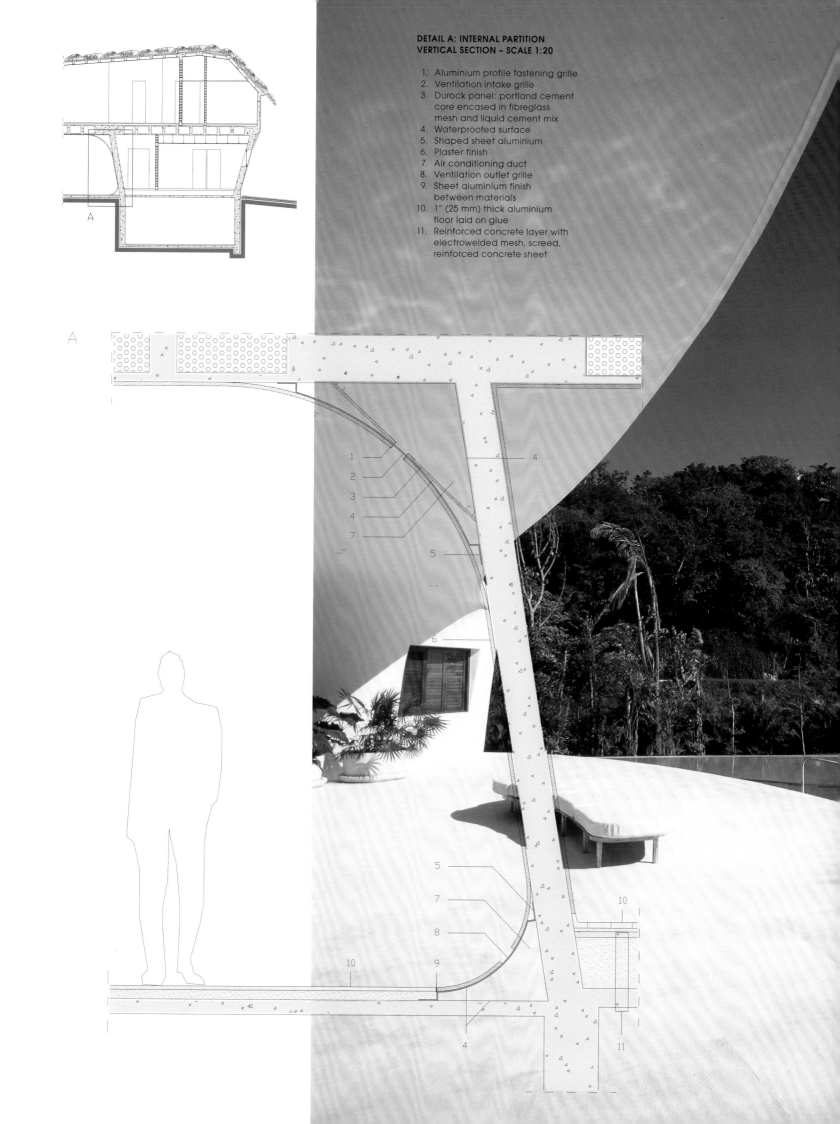

**DETAIL A: INTERNAL PARTITION
VERTICAL SECTION – SCALE 1:20**

1. Aluminium profile fastening grille
2. Ventilation intake grille
3. Durock panel: portland cement core encased in fibreglass mesh and liquid cement mix
4. Waterproofed surface
5. Shaped sheet aluminium
6. Plaster finish
7. Air conditioning duct
8. Ventilation outlet grille
9. Sheet aluminium finish between materials
10. 1" (25 mm) thick aluminium floor laid on glue
11. Reinforced concrete layer with electrowelded mesh, screed, reinforced concrete sheet

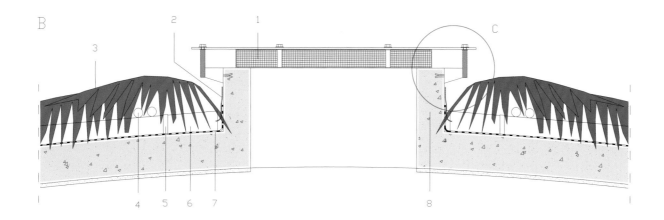

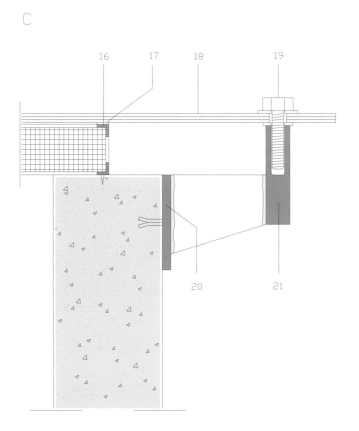

**DETAILS B AND C: SKYLIGHT AND ROOF
VERTICAL SECTIONS
SCALE 1:20 AND 1:5**

1. Stainless steel fly screen
2. Anodized sheet steel flashing
3. Roof formed by local palm leaves
4. Sticks binding palm leaves
5. Steel omega profile supporting roof
6. Load-bearing Ø 4" (100 mm) treated hard wood beam
7. Waterproofing membrane
8. Reinforced concrete edging supporting skylight
9. 15 3/4" (400 mm) reinforced concrete slab with polystyrene aggregate
10. Plaster finish
11. 3/4" (20 mm) drip moulding
12. Reinforced concrete edging, neoprene joint
13. Gypsum board finish
14. Wood door with 3/8" (9 mm) double glazing
15. Porcelain stone floor
16. Perimeter frame of 1/2 x 1/2"(12 x 12 mm) aluminium angle profiles
17. Neoprene joint
18. Skylight formed by two 1/4" (6.35 mm) tempered glass sheets separated by solar film
19. Stainless steel bolt fixing glass sheet
20. Structure of 3/8" (9.53 mm) steel plates with rust-proofing paint and three layers of enamel
21. Steel fixing plate

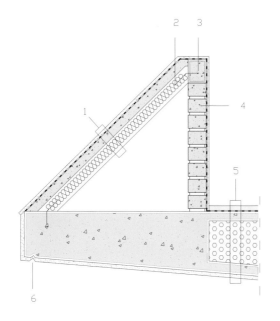

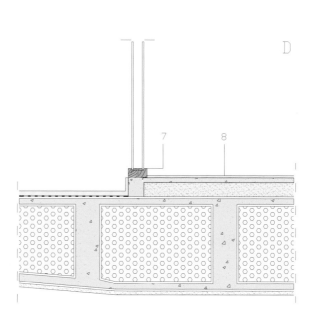

DETAIL D: TERRACE
VERTICAL SECTION – SCALE 1:20

1. Plaster finish, waterproofing membrane, reinforced concrete slab, board insulation
2. Board insulation support formed by 6 1/4" (160 mm) and 1/16" (2 mm) thick steel stirrups
3. Parapet in 4" (100 mm) thick concrete blocks
4. Cement and sand render
5. Floor formed by white concrete with washed pebble aggregate, waterproofing membrane, 15 3/4" (400 mm) reinforced concrete slab with polystyrene aggregate
6. 3/4" (20 mm) drip moulding
7. Wooden sliding door with 3/8 – 2 – 3/8" (9 – 50 – 9 mm) double glazing
8. Porcelain stone floor

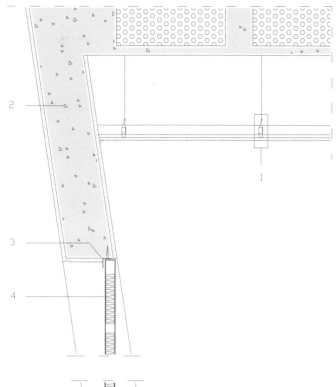
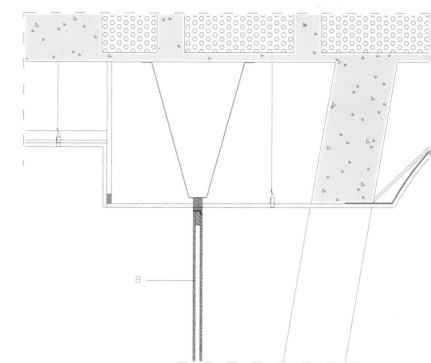
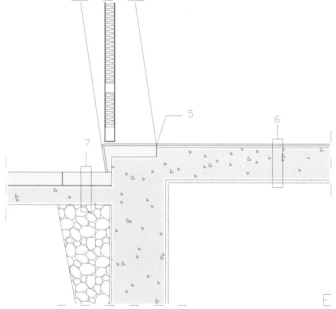

DETAIL E: KITCHEN
VERTICAL SECTION – SCALE 1:20

1. Gypsum board finish on substructure of steel C-profiles with metal tie rod supports
2. Reinforced concrete structure
3. 3/16" (5 mm) aluminium angle profile
4. Aluminium door with board

insulation and substructure in aluminium box profiles
5. 1/4" (6 mm) and 1/8" (3 mm) thick sheet aluminium joint
6. Porcelain stone floor, screed, reinforced concrete slab, plaster
7. Floor laid onsite, reinforced concrete slab, ballast
8. Wood door with wood infill

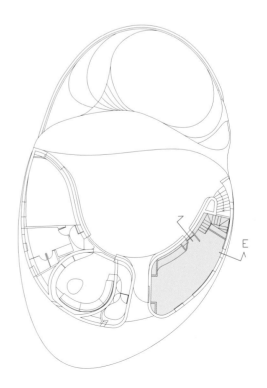

TWO HOUSES – PONTE DE LIMA, PORTUGAL
EDUARDO SOUTO DE MOURA

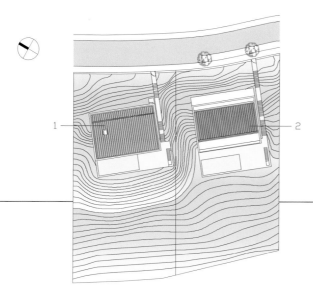

The architecture of Eduardo Souto de Moura is thoughtful, fraught with the doubts that assailed design and construction, yet at the same time rational, acknowledging contradictions and contrasts. The two detached residences with swimming pool at Ponte de Lima are a case in point. They represent two contrasting approaches to building on high-constraint terrain – here a steep slope.

As parallelepiped volumes, the two buildings are similar. Yet they are diametrically opposed. One house cantilevers out over the slope, standing out in stark relief; the other slides sleekly down the steep hill, parallel to the slope. But the contrast is not only about relating differently to natural surrounds. The houses are studies in "liveability". Each responds to different requirements: one takes in the surrounding landscape through wide, full-height glazed façades that give access to covered terraces protected only by simple metal railings; the other turns inward, in compliance with the client's desire for privacy, providing light exposure and views onto the outside from behind protective perimeter walls.

Both houses are connected to their respective road entrances by a flight of granite steps that continue down the slope along the sheer south wall of each building to the swimming pool and relaxation area.

The cantilevered house is a linear, single-storey construction. The ground floorplate connects to the foundations via a series of obliquely set slabs. The recessed east-facing entrance façade comprises a lower band of marble cladding, topped by a long glazed strip set in a stainless steel frame. The entrance gives directly into the day zone, with ample views over the landscape through sliding double-glazed panels supported by aluminium frames. The west section is divided in two by a transverse partition separating the living room from the four bedrooms. The galvanized sheet-steel-clad roof has a much gentler pitch than its neighbour's. The second house follows a more "natural" programme. But although hugging the slope in apparent simple obedience to the lay of the land, the architecture creates a series of different levels of its own. The building springs from foundations that intersect with the slope, allowing the westward thrust of the floorplate. As the focus is on secluded interior space, the ample glazed façades do not form the outermost perimeter of the building.

On the side overlooking the swimming pool, an open-sky enclosed terrace lets air and light into the double-height living area and bedrooms through a long glazed façade which, like its counterpart in the other house, gives a unifying appearance to the elevation. The accent though is on the legibility of the interiors washed by the slanting light, of the connections set up in the two-level plan, and the exterior landscape mediated by a screening wall. The double-height living room receives light from both sides. An elegant staircase with coloured granite steps cantilevers down the east wall. The steeply pitched, copper-clad roof is a core architectural feature.

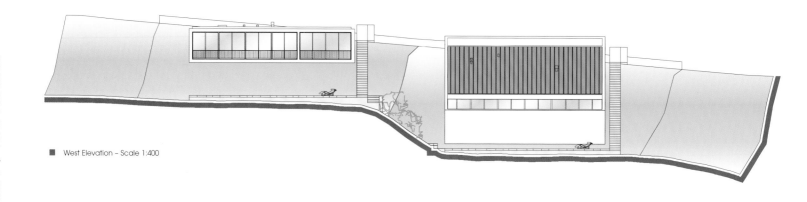

■ West Elevation – Scale 1:400

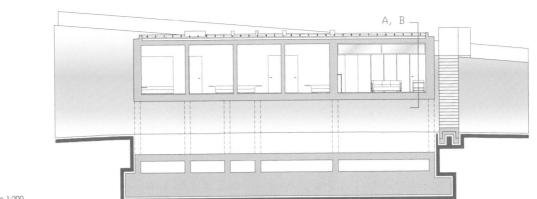

■ **House 1**
XX Section – Scale 1:200

■ **House 1**
YY Section – Scale 1:200

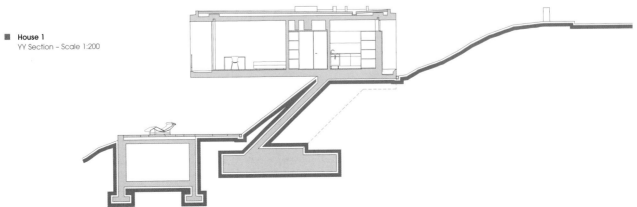

1. Entrance
2. Living-dining room
3. Kitchen
4. Dressing room
5. Bedroom
6. Bathroom
7. Terrace
8. Swimming pool
9. Garden

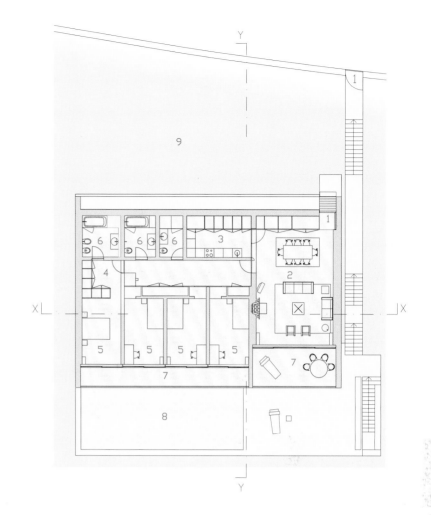

■ House 2
Kitchen/Dining Room Floor Plan – Scale 1:300

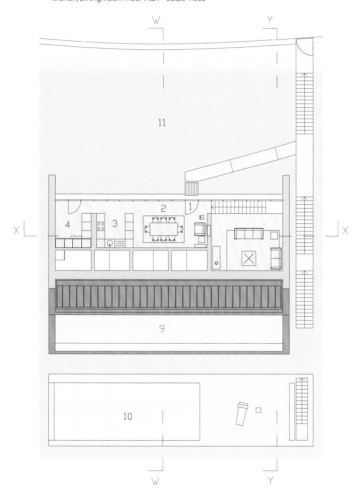

1. Entrance
2. Dining room
3. Kitchen
4. Laundry
5. Living room
6. Bedroom
7. Dressing room
8. Bathroom
9. Terrace
10. Swimming pool
11. Garden

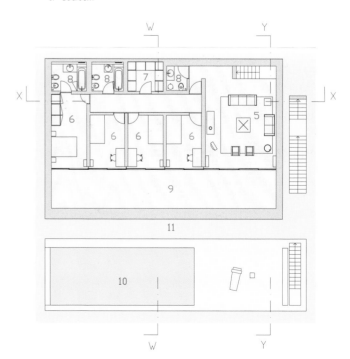

■ House 2
Living/Bedrooms Floor Plan – Scale 1:200

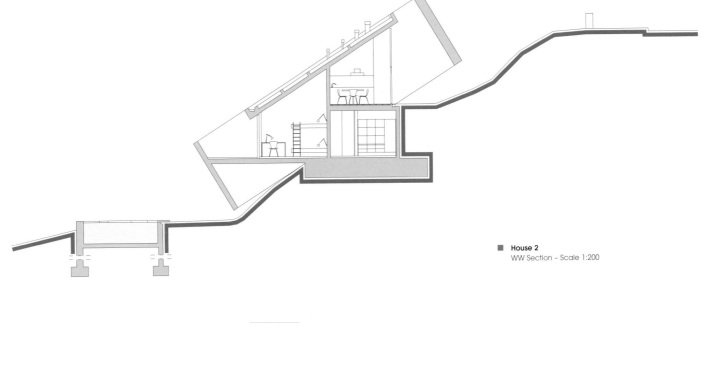

■ **House 2**
WW Section – Scale 1:200

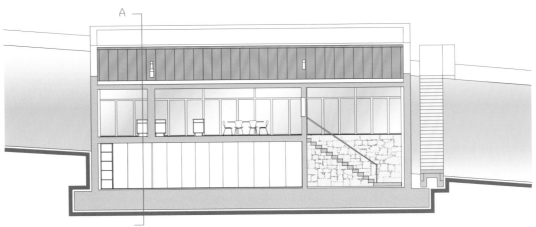

■ **House 2**
XX Section – Scale 1:200

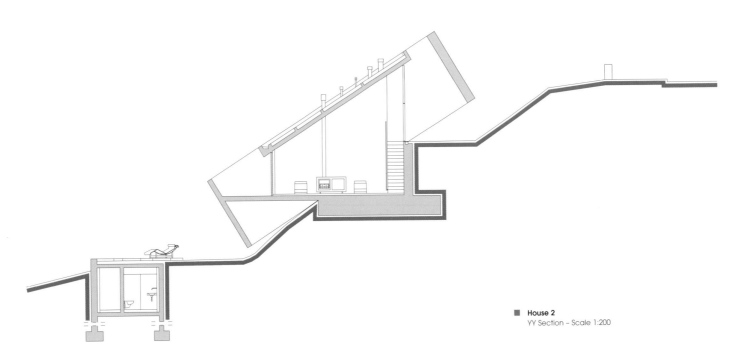

■ **House 2**
YY Section – Scale 1:200

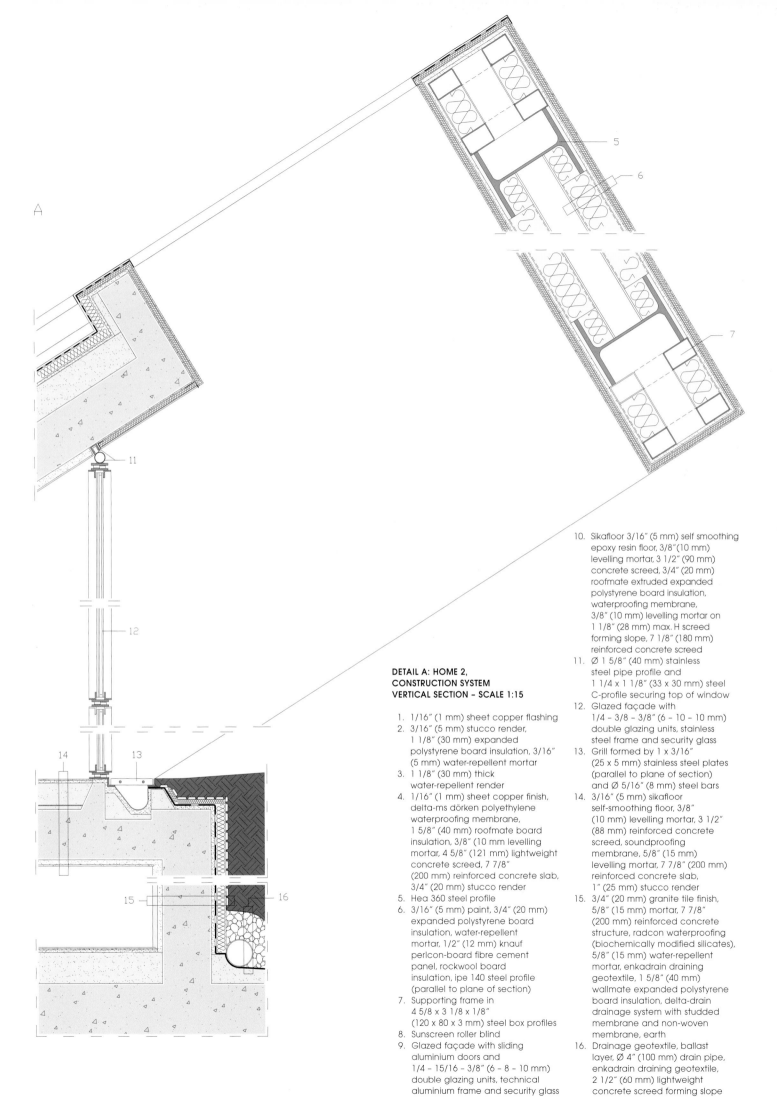

A

DETAIL A: HOME 2,
CONSTRUCTION SYSTEM
VERTICAL SECTION – SCALE 1:15

1. 1/16" (1 mm) sheet copper flashing
2. 3/16" (5 mm) stucco render, 1 1/8" (30 mm) expanded polystyrene board insulation, 3/16" (5 mm) water-repellent mortar
3. 1 1/8" (30 mm) thick water-repellent render
4. 1/16" (1 mm) sheet copper finish, delta-ms dörken polyethylene waterproofing membrane, 1 5/8" (40 mm) roofmate board insulation, 3/8" (10 mm) levelling mortar, 4 5/8" (121 mm) lightweight concrete screed, 7 7/8" (200 mm) reinforced concrete slab, 3/4" (20 mm) stucco render
5. Hea 360 steel profile
6. 3/16" (5 mm) paint, 3/4" (20 mm) expanded polystyrene board insulation, water-repellent mortar, 1/2" (12 mm) knauf perlcon-board fibre cement panel, rockwool board insulation, ipe 140 steel profile (parallel to plane of section)
7. Supporting frame in 4 5/8 x 3 1/8 x 1/8" (120 x 80 x 3 mm) steel box profiles
8. Sunscreen roller blind
9. Glazed façade with sliding aluminium doors and 1/4 – 15/16 – 3/8" (6 – 8 – 10 mm) double glazing units, technical aluminium frame and security glass

10. Sikafloor 3/16" (5 mm) self smoothing epoxy resin floor, 3/8"(10 mm) levelling mortar, 3 1/2" (90 mm) concrete screed, 3/4" (20 mm) roofmate extruded expanded polystyrene board insulation, waterproofing membrane, 3/8" (10 mm) levelling mortar on 1 1/8" (28 mm) max. H screed forming slope, 7 1/8" (180 mm) reinforced concrete screed
11. Ø 1 5/8" (40 mm) stainless steel pipe profile and 1 1/4 x 1 1/8" (33 x 30 mm) steel C-profile securing top of window
12. Glazed façade with 1/4 – 3/8 – 3/8" (6 – 10 – 10 mm) double glazing units, stainless steel frame and security glass
13. Grill formed by 1 x 3/16" (25 x 5 mm) stainless steel plates (parallel to plane of section) and Ø 5/16" (8 mm) steel bars
14. 3/16" (5 mm) sikafloor self-smoothing floor, 3/8" (10 mm) levelling mortar, 3 1/2" (88 mm) reinforced concrete screed, soundproofing membrane, 5/8" (15 mm) levelling mortar, 7 7/8" (200 mm) reinforced concrete slab, 1" (25 mm) stucco render
15. 3/4" (20 mm) granite tile finish, 5/8" (15 mm) mortar, 7 7/8" (200 mm) reinforced concrete structure, radcon waterproofing (biochemically modified silicates), 5/8" (15 mm) water-repellent mortar, enkadrain draining geotextile, 1 5/8" (40 mm) wallmate expanded polystyrene board insulation, delta-drain drainage system with studded membrane and non-woven membrane, earth
16. Drainage geotextile, ballast layer, Ø 4" (100 mm) drain pipe, enkadrain draining geotextile, 2 1/2" (60 mm) lightweight concrete screed forming slope

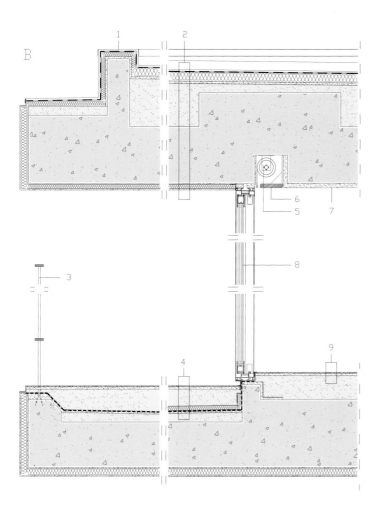

**DETAILS B AND C: HOME 1,
WESTERN AND EASTERN FAÇADES
VERTICAL SECTIONS – SCALE 1:15**

1. 1/16" (1 mm) galvanized sheet steel flashing
2. 1/16" (1 mm) galvanized sheet steel cladding, delta-ms dörken polyethylene waterproofing membrane, 1 5/8" (40 mm) roofmate extruded expanded polystyrene board insulation, 3/8" (10 mm) levelling mortar, 7 1/2" (192 mm) lightweight concrete screed, 9 7/8" (250 mm) reinforced concrete slab, 3/16" (5 mm) water-repellent mortar, 1 1/8" (30 mm) expanded polystyrene board insulation, 3/16" (5 mm) render
3. Parapet formed by in Ø 3/8" (10 mm) stainless steel bars
4. 3/16" (5 mm) sikafloor self-smoothing epoxy resin floor, 3/8" (10 mm) mortar, 3" (75 mm) concrete screed, 3/4" (20 mm) roofmate board insulation, waterproofing membrane, 3/8" (10 mm) levelling mortar on 1 3/4" (48 mm) max. H screed creating slope

5. Sunscreen roller blind
6. 5/8" (15 mm) plywood panel
7. 3/4" (20 mm) stucco render
8. Glazed façade with sliding aluminium doors with 1/4 – 5/16 – 3/8" (6 – 8 – 10.2 mm) double glazing technical aluminium frame and security glass
9. 3/16" (5 mm) sikafloor self-smoothing epoxy resin floor, 3/8" (10 mm) levelling mortar, 3 1/8" (80 mm) concrete screed
10. Fixed window with stainless steel frame and 1/8 – 5/16 – 5/16" (4 – 8 – 8 mm) double glazing
11. 1 1/8" (30 mm) thick marble cladding (parallel to plane of section)
12. Door formed by stainless sheet steel and 2 1/2" (59 mm) high-density rockwool
13. 1 1/8" (30 mm) steel grille, 2 1/8" (54 mm) porous concrete screed, Ø 1 3/4" (46 mm) steel drain pipe, drainage geotextile, 3/4" (20 mm) roofmate board insulation, waterproofing membrane, 3/8" (10 mm) levelling mortar on 2" (50 mm) max. H screed creating slope
14. 8 1/8" (205 mm) granite step, 2" (50 mm) gravel layer, ballast

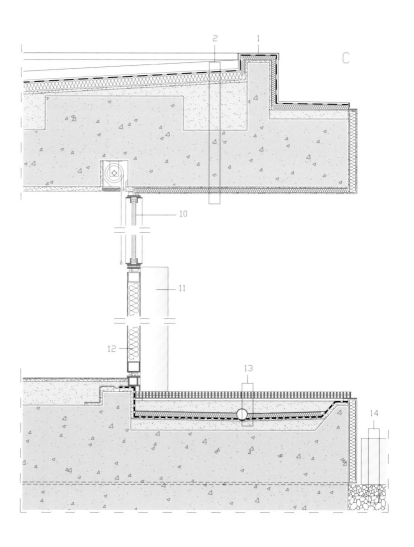

■ Ground Floor Plan – Scale 1:250

1. Entrance
2. Kitchen
3. Back entrance
4. Dining room
5. Study
6. Living room
7. Bedroom
8. Entertainment
9. Terrace

■ First Floor Plan – Scale 1:250

For this project at Tarcento (near Udine), the Geza studio (Gri e Zucchi Associati) started with a site containing a number of largish buildings of mixed early twentieth-century styles. The brief was to fit an extension on the master-building, landscape the open ground and put in a new garage on the sloping hillside. The ground is partly flat and partly on a steep slope. The three constructions on it were the master-building, an outbuilding and a greenhouse. The challenge with the extension was how to blend the notion of connecting to, yet differentiating from, the pre-existing four-square building. Once the outhouses appended to the main house had been demolished, and the latter fully restored, the design task was to highlight the contrast of the new addition while giving rhythm to the various elevations. The new architectural addition connects directly onto the historical building along its eastern wall. Its visible walls are painted unconventional black to contrast with the white of the old part.

A staircase was put in at the junction of the two units, using different materials to lighten the effect: the first flight in local stone, the others in a steel structure with wooden treads. Where the extension joins the main building, the different character of the two architectural styles is made into a feature. The contemporary speaks a language of its own, its materials sharply defined. One device employed in the project is to set back the north and south frontages from the line of the old construction so as to emphasize the distinction, not let the extension perimeter interfere with the compact pre-existing shape, and not create difficulties of join between walls and corners of the buildings. The geometrical stiffness of the former architectural style contrasts with the varied look of the new wing and its elevations. Broad full-length glass walls give light to the interior and link strongly to the surrounding context. A double "T" section beam runs lengthwise across the façade onto which a terraced area opens out, breaking up the regular line. The original design of the chimneys forms an architectural motif. Variety is also built into the cladding of the walls: Rheinzink panels, wood, black render. Floor heights are kept the same between the two buildings. The gable roof, panelled in Rheinzink, follows the line of the outbuilding opposite.

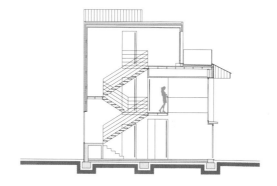

■ West Elevation – Scale 1:250

■ XX Longitudinal Section – Scale 1:200

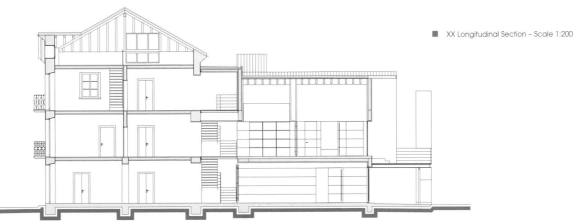

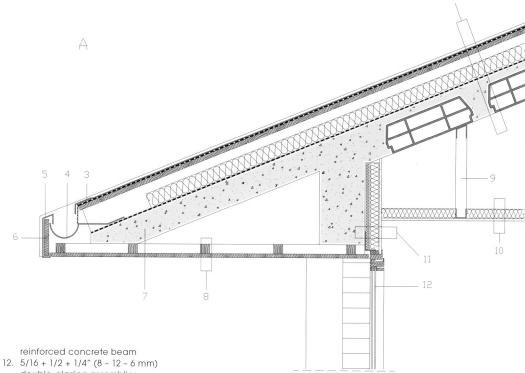

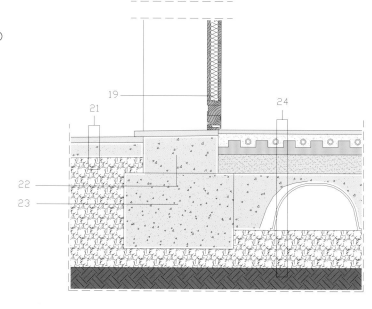

DETAILS A AND B: EXTENSION FAÇADES
VERTICAL SECTIONS – SCALE 1:20

1. Rheinzink sheet cladding on 23% slope, waterproofing membrane, 1" (25 mm) pine plank, 2" (50 mm) airspace and timber beams (orthogonal to plane of section), 3 1/8" (80 mm) rigid board insulation, vapour barrier, 6 1/4 + 1 5/8" (160 + 40 mm) concrete and masonry roof
2. Rheinzink sheet cladding on 27% slope, waterproofing membrane, 1" (25 mm) pine plank, 2" (50 mm) airspace and timber beams (orthogonal to plane of section), 3 1/8" (80 mm) board insulation, vapour barrier, 1" (25 mm) pine plank, wooden beam painted white (parallel to plane of section)
3. Steel insect guard
4. Rheinzink guttering
5. Rheinzink flashing
6. 1" (25 mm) thick pine edge slat
7. Reinforced concrete beam
8. 3/4" (20 mm) mahogany panel, 2 x 2" (50 x 50 mm) wood battens
9. Frame in aluminium C-profiles supporting suspended ceiling
10. Suspended ceiling in 1/2" (12.5 mm) gypsum board panels, 2" (50 mm) rockwool insulation
11. 1/2" (12.5 mm) gypsum board panel, 2" (50 mm) rockwool insulation, 1" (25 mm) insulation, steel i-profile supporting insulation,

reinforced concrete beam
12. 5/16 + 1/2 + 1/4" (8 – 12 – 6 mm) double-glazing assemblies with wood frames
13. Motorized sliding mahogany panel
14. Marble window sill
15. Screed
16. 3/4" (20 mm) merbau wood parquetry flooring, 2" (50 mm) screed, 3 1/2" (90 mm) insulating lightweight concrete, 6 1/4 + 1 5/8" (160 + 40 mm) concrete and masonry floor
17. Maintenance parapet formed by double T-section steel beam
18. 3/4" (20 mm) plaster painted black, 2" (50 mm) mineralized wood panel, reinforced concrete beam
19. Infilled window in mahogany
20. Wooden sliding door with 5/16 – 1/2 – 5/16" (8 – 14 – 8 mm) double glazing
21. External paving in 1 1/8" (30 mm) washed concrete on 1% slope, 2 3/4" (70 mm) reinforced concrete screed, lean concrete
22. Reinforced concrete footing
23. Reinforced concrete foundation
24. Internal flooring in 3/4" (20 mm) slate tiles, screed on radiant panel, 4" (100 mm) insulating lightweight concrete, reinforced concrete screed, ventilation space with plastic elements, lean concrete, earth
25. External paving in 1 1/8" (30 mm) washed concrete on 1% slope, sand, 2 1/2" (60 mm) reinforced concrete screed, lean concrete, earth

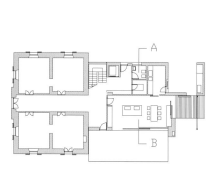

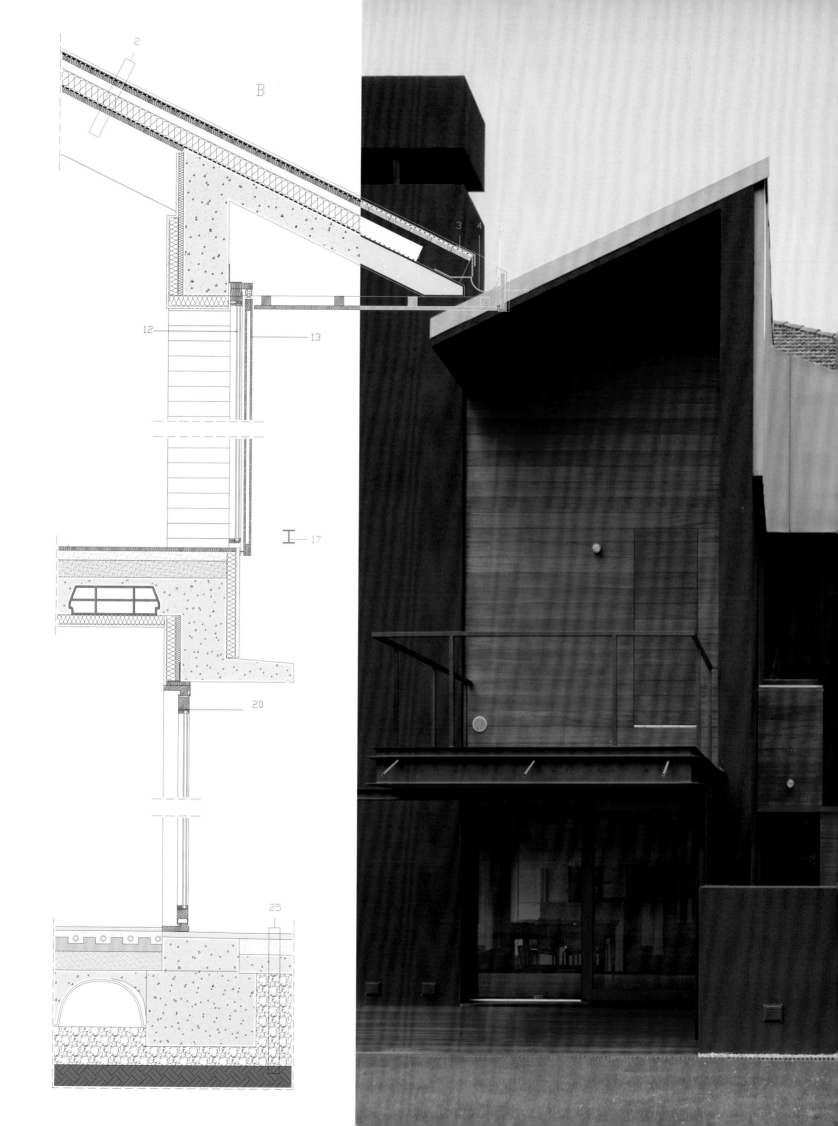

2

B

3 4 5

12

13

17

20

25

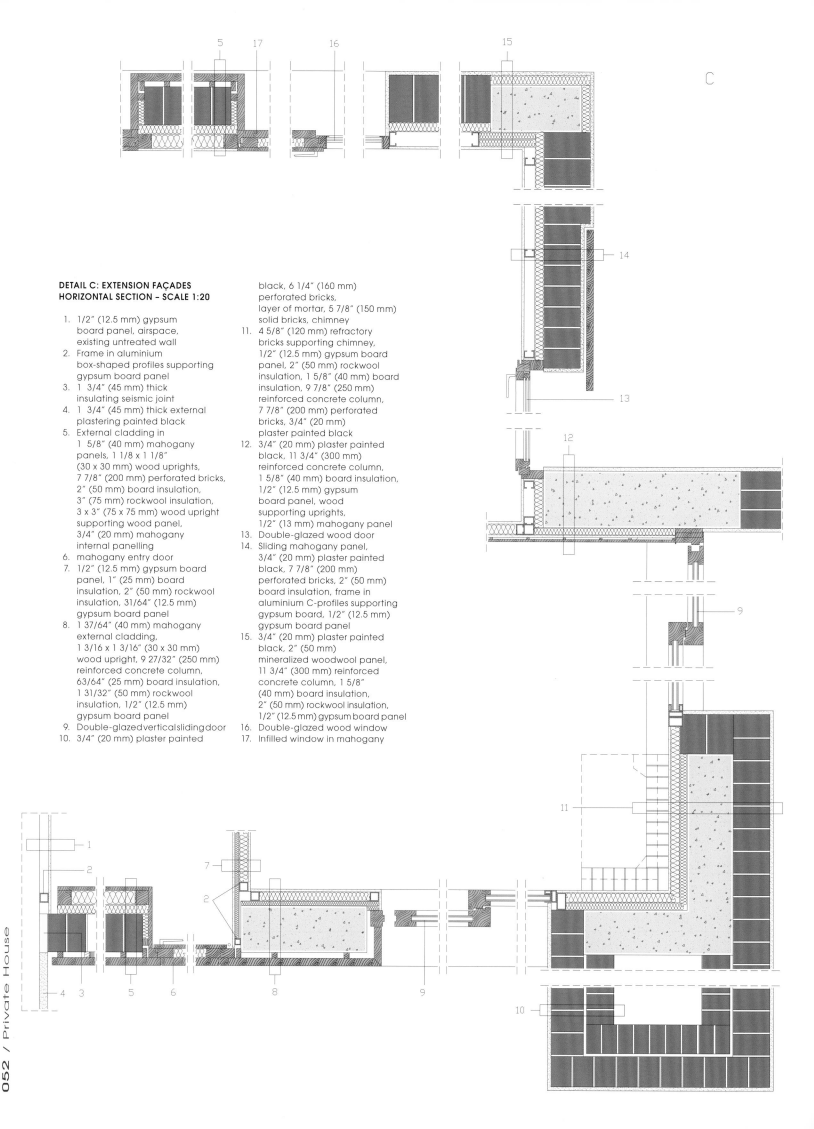

DETAIL C: EXTENSION FAÇADES
HORIZONTAL SECTION – SCALE 1:20

1. 1/2" (12.5 mm) gypsum board panel, airspace, existing untreated wall
2. Frame in aluminium box-shaped profiles supporting gypsum board panel
3. 1 3/4" (45 mm) thick insulating seismic joint
4. 1 3/4" (45 mm) thick external plastering painted black
5. External cladding in 1 5/8" (40 mm) mahogany panels, 1 1/8 x 1 1/8" (30 x 30 mm) wood uprights, 7 7/8" (200 mm) perforated bricks, 2" (50 mm) board insulation, 3" (75 mm) rockwool insulation, 3 x 3" (75 x 75 mm) wood upright supporting wood panel, 3/4" (20 mm) mahogany internal panelling
6. mahogany entry door
7. 1/2" (12.5 mm) gypsum board panel, 1" (25 mm) board insulation, 2" (50 mm) rockwool insulation, 31/64" (12.5 mm) gypsum board panel
8. 1 37/64" (40 mm) mahogany external cladding, 1 3/16 x 1 3/16" (30 x 30 mm) wood upright, 9 27/32" (250 mm) reinforced concrete column, 63/64" (25 mm) board insulation, 1 31/32" (50 mm) rockwool insulation, 1/2" (12.5 mm) gypsum board panel
9. Double-glazed vertical sliding door
10. 3/4" (20 mm) plaster painted black, 6 1/4" (160 mm) perforated bricks, layer of mortar, 5 7/8" (150 mm) solid bricks, chimney
11. 4 5/8" (120 mm) refractory bricks supporting chimney, 1/2" (12.5 mm) gypsum board panel, 2" (50 mm) rockwool insulation, 1 5/8" (40 mm) board insulation, 9 7/8" (250 mm) reinforced concrete column, 7 7/8" (200 mm) perforated bricks, 3/4" (20 mm) plaster painted black
12. 3/4" (20 mm) plaster painted black, 11 3/4" (300 mm) reinforced concrete column, 1 5/8" (40 mm) board insulation, 1/2" (12.5 mm) gypsum board panel, wood supporting uprights, 1/2" (13 mm) mahogany panel
13. Double-glazed wood door
14. Sliding mahogany panel, 3/4" (20 mm) plaster painted black, 7 7/8" (200 mm) perforated bricks, 2" (50 mm) board insulation, frame in aluminium C-profiles supporting gypsum board, 1/2" (12.5 mm) gypsum board panel
15. 3/4" (20 mm) plaster painted black, 2" (50 mm) mineralized woodwool panel, 11 3/4" (300 mm) reinforced concrete column, 1 5/8" (40 mm) board insulation, 2" (50 mm) rockwool insulation, 1/2" (12.5 mm) gypsum board panel
16. Double-glazed wood window
17. Infilled window in mahogany

SUMMER HOUSE – ZAPALLAR, CHILE
ENRIQUE BROWNE & ARQUITECTOS ASOCIADOS

■ Site Plan – Scale 1:1000

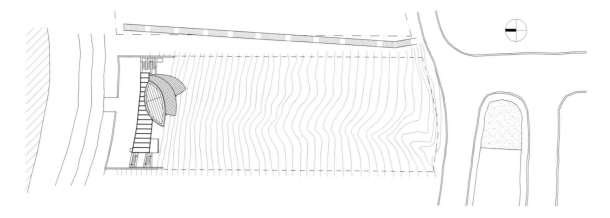

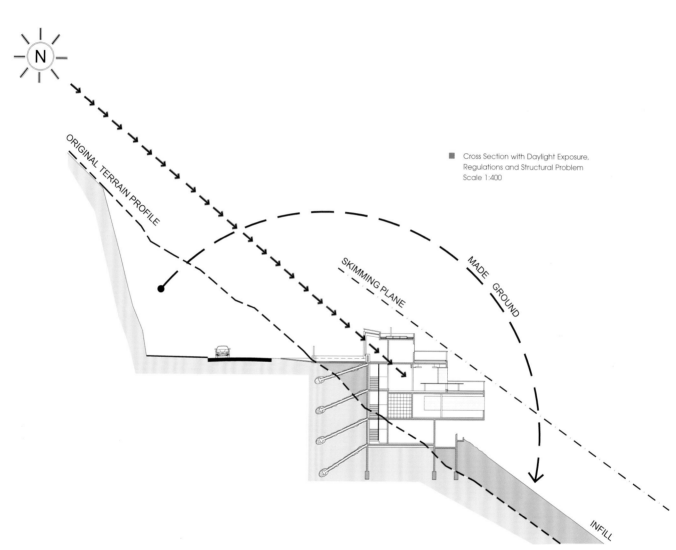

N

ORIGINAL TERRAIN PROFILE

■ Cross Section with Daylight Exposure,
Regulations and Structural Problem
Scale 1:400

MADE GROUND

SKIMMING PLANE

INFILL

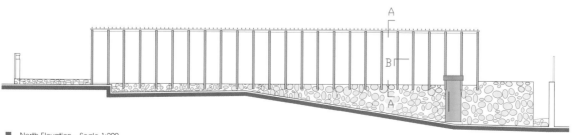

A

B

A

■ North Elevation – Scale 1:200

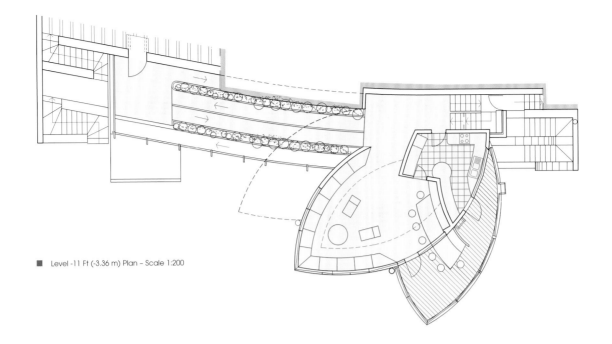

■ Level -11 Ft (-3.36 m) Plan – Scale 1:200

The house is located on a long, narrow, fairly steep plot running north-south, with a highway passing along its upper perimeter and a street bordering its southern extremity. The upper storeys provide splendid views of the beach and bay. The terrain presented two problems: firstly, its southward projection means it receives very little sunlight and, secondly, regulations oblige a maximum elevation of 24.6 Ft (7.5 m) from the ground. Hence the decision to locate the house on the highest point, as close to the highway as possible, and create a series of distinct volumes following the natural gradient so as to exploit this regulation to the full, thus maximizing natural light and views.

The highway-facing façade comprises translucent thermal glazing that glows at night like a long horizontal lamp. The building itself literally "bursts out" over the slope. Depending on your angle of view, the house either seems to hover above its plot or is part of the wooded landscape with its outer coating of oxidized copper.

Made up of three superimposed "boats" or "leaves" set at different angles and linked together by glass-covered ramps, this zigzagging configuration offers a variety of views of both the house itself and the town. The main bedroom is at the top of the house, the living, dining room, kitchen area on the intermediate level, while the children's rooms are on the bottom. Volume distribution has been designed to suggest a branch with green leaves.

Although certain formal aspects may seem arbitrary at first sight, they are absolutely necessary: the north-facing translucent thermal glazing overlooking the road lets in the winter daylight while excluding noise; the descending array of superimposed "boats" provides a series of different views and allows elevation to 24.6 Ft (7.5 m) throughout.

The stone and green patina-covered copper blend the building with its natural environment. The stone is typical of the Zapallar area while copper is Chile's main export product.

■ Level -20 Ft (-6.03 m) Plan – Scale 1:200

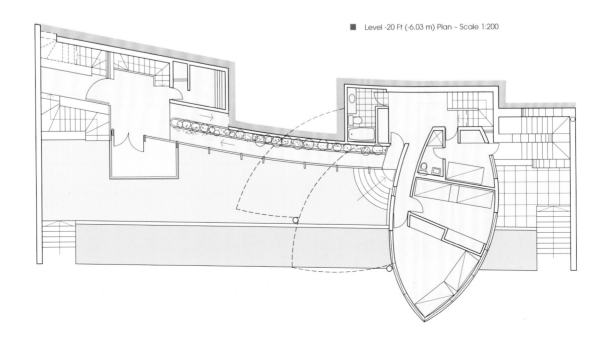

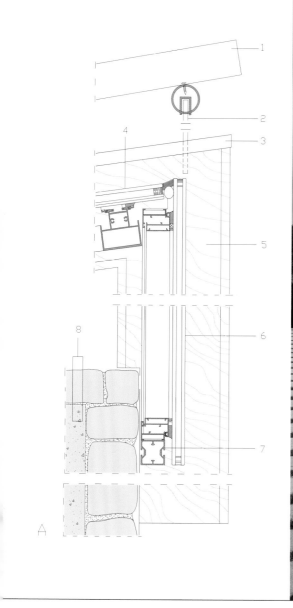

A

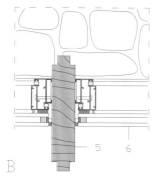

B

**DETAILS A AND B: GLAZED FAÇADE
VERTICAL AND HORIZONTAL
SECTIONS – SCALE 1:10**

1. 3 3/4 x 3/4" (94 x 20 mm) aluminium
   box-shaped profile painted white
2. Supporting structure in
   Ø 3 1/8" (78 mm) aluminium
   pipe profiles and 1 3/4 x 1 1/4"
   (48 x 31 mm) coupled aluminium
   C-profiles on 1/2" (12.5 mm)
   aluminium plate (parallel
   to plane of section)
3. Sheet aluminium flashing
   (parallel to plane of section)
4. Roof with 3/8 – 3/4 – 1/2"

(9 – 18 – 13 mm) aluminium
   double-glazing assembly
5. 12" (306 mm) laminated
   wood column (parallel
   to plane of section)
6. Glazed façade with
   3/8 – 5/8 – 3/8" (10 – 15 – 10 mm)
   low-emissivity glass, aluminium
   double-glazing units with
   sandblasted exterior
7. Section of frame with space
   for rainwater runoff
8. 5 5/8" (143 mm) stone cladding,
   reinforced concrete structure

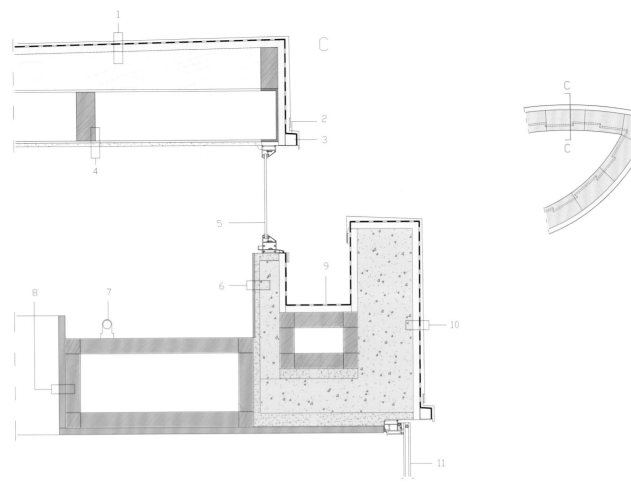

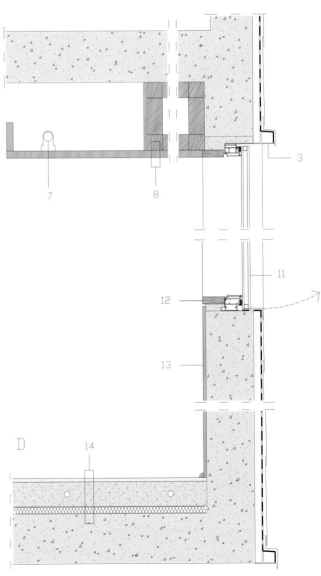

**DETAILS C AND D:
CONSTRUCTION SYSTEM
OF PETALS – SCALE 1:10**

1. Roof with 1/16" (2 mm) green
   patinated copper covering,
   waterproofing membrane,
   3/4" (19 mm) phenolic orientated
   strandboard panel, frame
   of wood beams (parallel
   to plane of section)
2. 1/16" (2 mm) copper sheeting
3. 1 1/8 x 1 1/8" (30 x 30 mm)
   aluminium box profile
   drip moulding
4. 3/8" (9 mm) gypsum board
   on frame of 5 1/2 x 1 3/4"
   (140 x 47 mm) steel C-profiles
   and 5 1/8 x 2 1/8" (129 x 57 mm)
   wood beams
5. Fixed window with 3/16" (5.5 mm)
   glass and aluminium frame
6. 1/4" (6 mm) veneered
   chipboard panelling,
   1/2" (14 mm) levelling mortar,
   2 1/8" (54 mm) pre-cast

concrete panel
7. White fluorescent light fitting
8. 3/4" (18 mm) manio wood-based
   upholstered plywood panel
   on frame of 1 5/8 x 1 5/8"
   (40 x 40 mm) wood beams
9. Rainwater gutter
10. 1/16" (2 mm) green patinated
    copper finish, waterproofing
    membrane, 3/4" (19 mm)
    phenolic orientated strandboard
    panel, 6 1/8" (153 mm)
    reinforced concrete edging
11. Sliding full-length glazed
    aluminium door with
    3/16 – 3/8 – 3/16" (5.5 – 9 – 5.5 mm)
    double glazing
12. 2 1/2 x 3/4" (60 x 20 mm)
    manio wood glazed door frame
13. 3/8" (9 mm) upholstered
    chipboard panel
14. 3/8" (10 mm) carpeting,
    2 3/4" (70 mm) lightweight
    concrete screed with radiant
    heating, 3/4" (20 mm)
    polystyrene board insulation

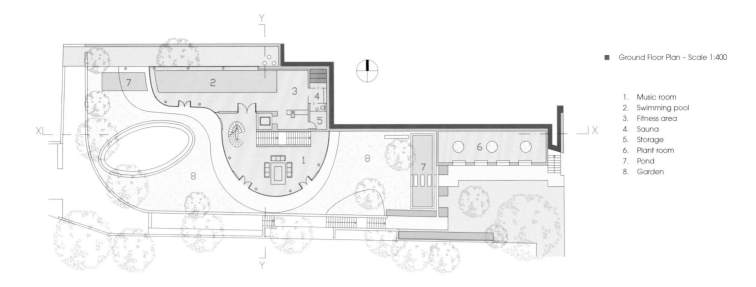

■ Ground Floor Plan – Scale 1:400

1. Music room
2. Swimming pool
3. Fitness area
4. Sauna
5. Storage
6. Plant room
7. Pond
8. Garden

The client, a German sailing and underwater photography enthusiast, held an anonymous international competition in 2001 which was won by the Reichel Architekten practice.

The Wellenhaus is an attempt to translate into a modern key Palladio's concept of "magnificence" and "grandeur" expressed in his *Four Books on Architecture*. The result is not so much a reproduction of the codified forms of the Palladian villa (stepped entrance, lateral service wings, and grand staircase), as a reinterpretation of the concept of "magnificence" in a contemporary context.

The portal entrance shelters the building without revealing anything of its interior. The open court is awash with vibrations from the surrounding building. From here a winding staircase gives access, at each bend, to the various garden levels, offering sweeping views of the surrounding Rhine valley countryside. Ideally connected to the Guggenheim of Frank Lloyd Wright in New York as a formal reference, Reichel has embedded the building in its natural setting. The gradient of the sloping terrain is a key element of the whole project, defining the building's geometry, the play of light and shadow of cantilevered elements and stacked levels, broad, curving surfaces and spiralled shapes.

The sinuous, harmonious flow of the façades of the Wellenhaus recalls the rolling waves of the sea. The parapets resemble the sides of a ship. The ground plan sets out to make interior and exterior spaces permeable. Wide glazed façades blur the line of demarcation between inside and out. The ground floor houses guest and custodian quarters, a projection room, service areas, cellar and garage. A continuum with the garden, the first floor contains a small concert hall, art collection exhibition area, swimming pool and fitness corner, each section flowing effortlessly into the next. The private apartments are on the upper floors. The last storey, housing the night quarters and library, provides stunning views as far as the eye can see.

The harmonious shades of the natural, unrendered materials lend the building a warm, quiet elegance. The walls, which seem to grow out of the ground, are in white-mix, fair-face concrete. The floors, some of which extend to the outside, are clad in light-coloured Spanish calcareous stone, as are some of the interior walls. The curved glazed frontage is regularly broken up by doors and mat finish steel panels with air vents for natural ventilation. The ample use of glazed façades has been compensated for with careful attention to energy saving.

■ First and Second Floor Plans – Scale 1:400

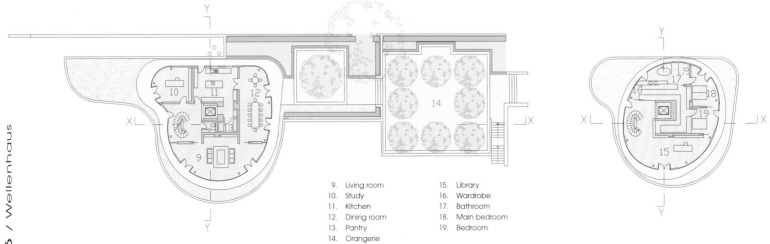

9. Living room
10. Study
11. Kitchen
12. Dining room
13. Pantry
14. Orangerie

15. Library
16. Wardrobe
17. Bathroom
18. Main bedroom
19. Bedroom

A

■ XX Section – Scale 1:250

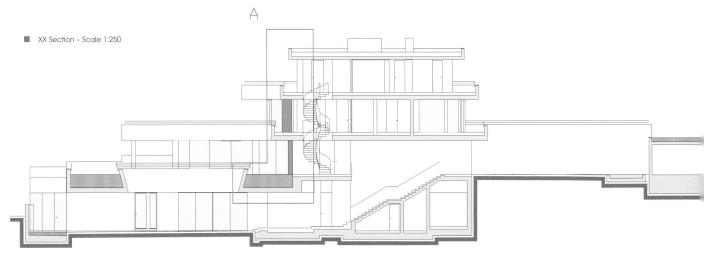

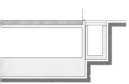

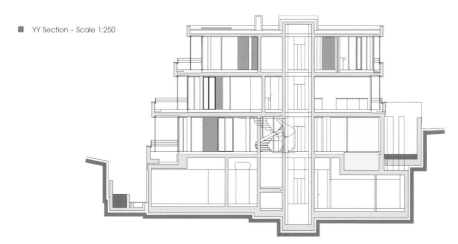

■ YY Section – Scale 1:250

DETAIL A: SOUTH-WEST FAÇADE
VERTICAL SECTION – SCALE 1:30

1. 1 1/8" (30 mm) thick white limestone coping
2. Bituminous sheath, 7 7/8" (200 mm) board insulation, 5 1/2" (140 mm) reinforced radiant concrete slab, 4" (100 mm) board insulation, suspended ceiling In 1/2" (12 mm) gypsum board
3. 1/16" (2 mm) water-repellent and anti-mould paint, 1/16" (2 mm) screed, 5/8" (16 mm) render, 9 7/8" (250 mm) reinforced concrete structure
4. 5 1/2 – 10 3/4" (140 – 275 mm) ballast
5. Flooring in 1 1/8" (30 mm) white limestone tiles, 1 1/8" (30 mm) layer of dry sand, 1 5/8" (42 mm) slab of self-draining concrete, 1/4" (7 mm) drainage sheath, double waterproofing membrane, 4" (100 mm) fibreglass board insulation, 2" (50 mm) insulation layer, 7 1/2 – 10 5/8" (190 – 270 mm) reinforced concrete slab, 4 1/4" (108 mm) board insulation, suspended ceiling in 1/2" (12 mm) gypsum board
6. Sliding sunblind in metal grating fitted in frame of anodized aluminium profiles
7. Flooring in 1 1/8" (30 mm) white limestone tiles, 1 1/8" (30 mm) layer of dry sand, 2 1/8" (55 mm) lightweight concrete screed with PVC radiant heating pipes, double 1 1/8 + 2 1/8" (30 + 55 mm) board insulation, vapour barrier, 11 3/4 - 15" (300 – 380 mm) reinforced concrete slab, 1 3/4" (48 mm) insulation layer, suspended ceiling in 1/2" (12 mm) acoustic gypsum board
8. 4 1/2 x 3" (115 x 75 cm) reinforced concrete beam
9. 4" (100 mm) fibreglass insulation around perimeter, 1/16" (2 mm) waterproofing membrane
10. Flooring in 1 1/8" (30 mm) white limestone tiles, 3/8" (10 mm) layer of dry sand, 10 5/8" (270 mm) slab of self-draining concrete on 1.1% slope, waterproofing membrane, 20 3/4" (525 mm) light layer of blond peat, double waterproofing sheath, double 4 + 4" (100 + 100 mm) board insulation, waterproofing membrane, 11 3/4" (300 mm) reinforced concrete slab, 3 1/2" (90 mm) board insulation, 1/16" (2 mm) screed, 1/16" (2 mm) water-repellent and anti-mould paint
11. Parapet in Ø 1 1/8" (30 mm) steel tubular profiles
12. 4 x 4 x 3/8" (100 x 100 x 10 mm) painted stainless steel plate supporting parapet
13. 1/16" (2 mm) water-repellent and anti-mould paint, 1/16" (2 mm) screed, 5/8"(16 mm) render, 11 3/8" (290 mm) reinforced concrete structure, double 1/16 + 1/16" (2 + 2 mm) waterproofing sheath, 1/16" (2 mm) render, 1/16" (2 mm) water-repellent and anti-mould paint

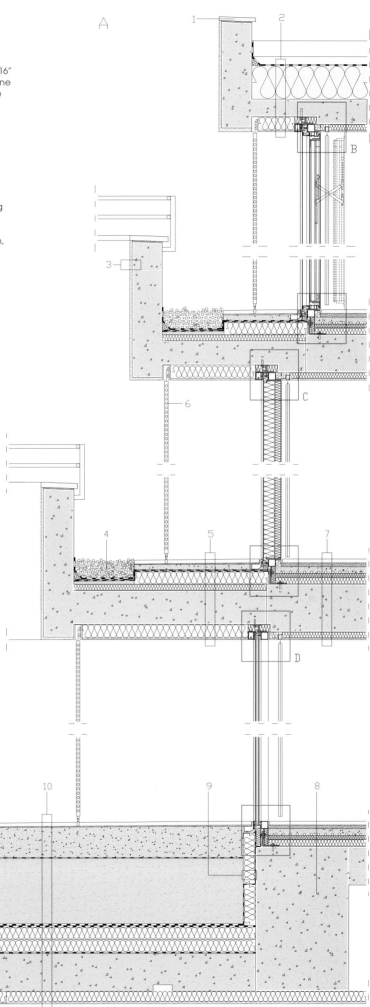

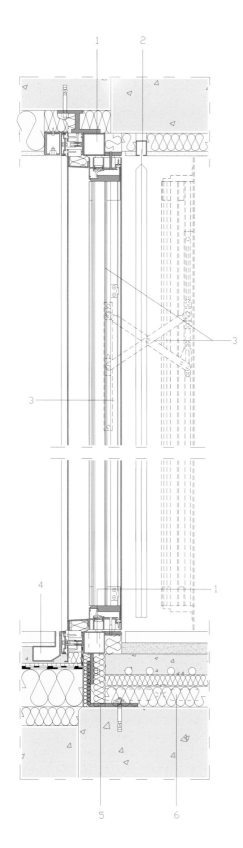

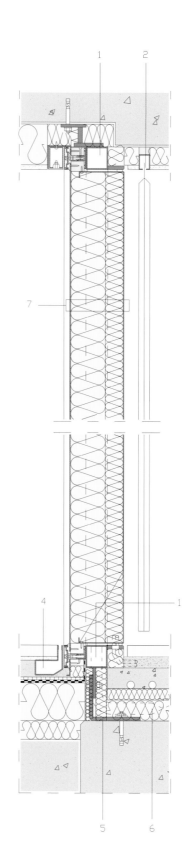

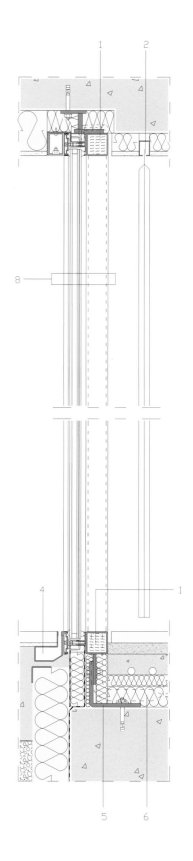

B

C

D

FAÇADE SYSTEM
DETAILS B, C AND D: VERTICAL SECTIONS
DETAIL E: HORIZONTAL SECTION –
SCALE 1:10

1. Glazed wall radiant heating
   system formed by 2 1/2 x 2 1/2"
   (60 x 60 mm) steel box-shaped
   profile forming cornice
   to glazing unit
2. 1 1/8" (30 mm) thick
   translucent silvered blind
3. Motorized ventilation opening

with grille connected to frame
by 10 3/4 x 3/4 x 1/8"
(277 x 20 x 4 mm) hinged
and sliding steel arms
4. 1 5/8 x 3" (40 x 75 mm)
   sheet aluminium drain
5. 4 x 4" (100 x 100 mm)
   steel I-shaped bracket
   attaching glazing unit to
   slab via expansion anchor
6. 1 1/8" (30 mm) Ø outlet duct
   for façade radiant heating
7. 1/8" (3 mm) sheet steel cladding,

3 3/4" (95 mm) board insulation,
2" (50 mm) acoustic insulation
panel, 1/8" (3 mm)
sheet steel cladding
8. Glazed wall formed by
   1/4 + 1/8 + 3/16 – 1/16 – 3/16"
   (6 + 4 + 5 – 1 – 5 mm) double
   glazing units with layer of krypton
   gas and double security glass,
   2 1/2 x 2 1/2" (60 x 60 mm)
   steel box-shaped profile
   (parallel to plane of section)
   forming cornice to glazing

unit for ducting heated air
9. 4 1/8 x 1 5/8 x 1/16"
   (105 x 40 x 2 mm) sheet
   aluminium frame covering
10. 2 1/2 x 2 1/2 x 5/16"
    (60 x 60 x 8 mm) steel T-shaped
    upright supporting glazed wall
11. Glazed door with
    aluminium frame and
    1/4 + 1/8 + 3/16 – 1/16 – 3/16"
    (6 + 4 + 5 – 1 – 5 mm) double
    glazing with layer of krypton
    gas and double security glass

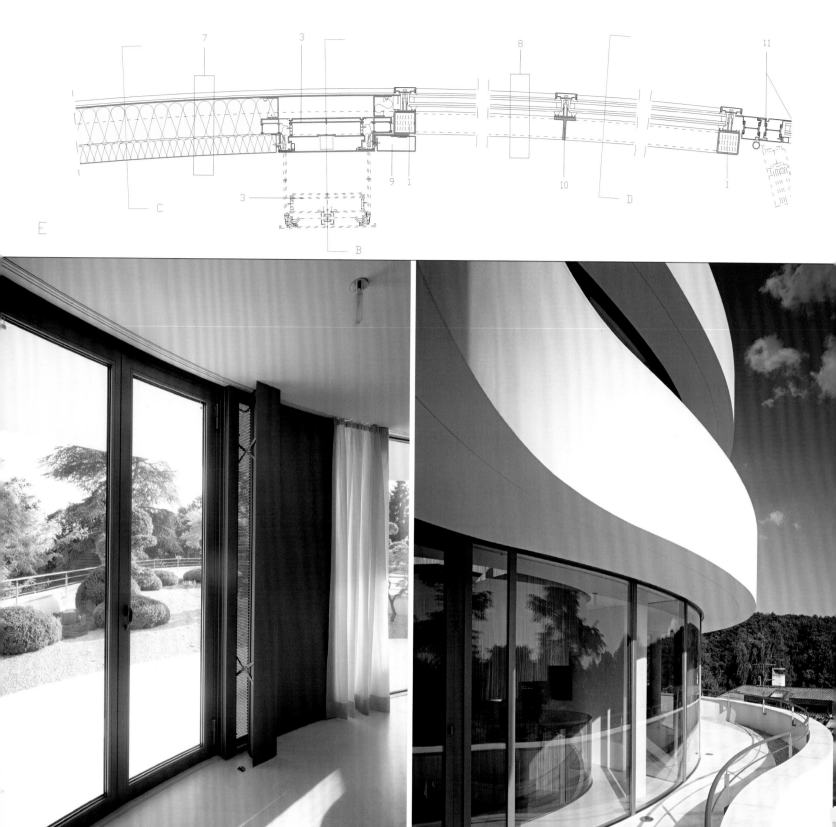

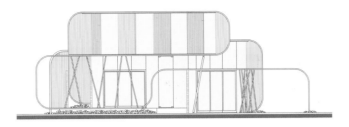

The Japanese avant-garde architect Shuhei Endo has long been engrossed with the subjects of geometrical form and its architectural development from simple to complex. His basic design idea develops out of the attempt to transform flat geometry into volume, via curvature and planar extension. The studio-dwelling called "Springtecture B" is remarkable for the simplicity of its materials: brick dividing walls in the classic earthenware shade or variants of white with black inserts; bare steel for the structure of diagonal cross-stays; glass and wood for the extra thick doors and windows; and everywhere sheet metal folding upon itself to form the roof, façade, walls and even floor.

The architect's own coinage, "Springtecture", puts its finger on his architectural style where form and volume spring from folded planes –

floors, walls, roofs – connected by natural curves. Made up of contrasts, the structure is designed in a series of arches meeting straight lines. The result is curvilinear yet planar at the same time.

Rooms peel off, sharing boundaries (inside/outside, front/back) and setting up a chain of continuous movement from outside to in and back again. Such architecture of partly shared features is called "Bunyutai" in Japanese. There is a sense of spaciousness about the rooms, despite their simplicity: architecture created out of its materials and the forms in which the architect chooses to employ them. The resultant studio-dwelling makes a strikingly theatrical play on minimalism: everything see-through, structure and roof.

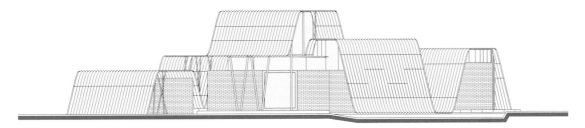

■ Ground Floor Plan – Scale 1:200

1. Parking
2. Entrance
3. Gallery
4. Rest space
5. Bedroom
6. Dining room
7. Terrace

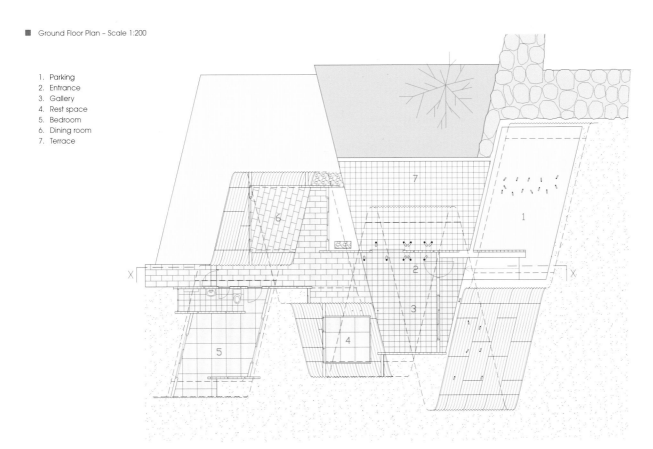

■ XX Section – Scale 1:200

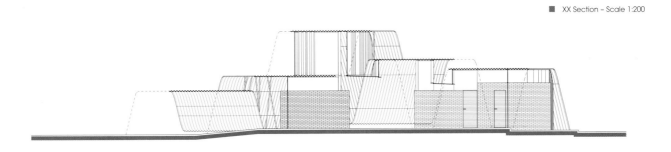

■ Different Developments of Springtecture

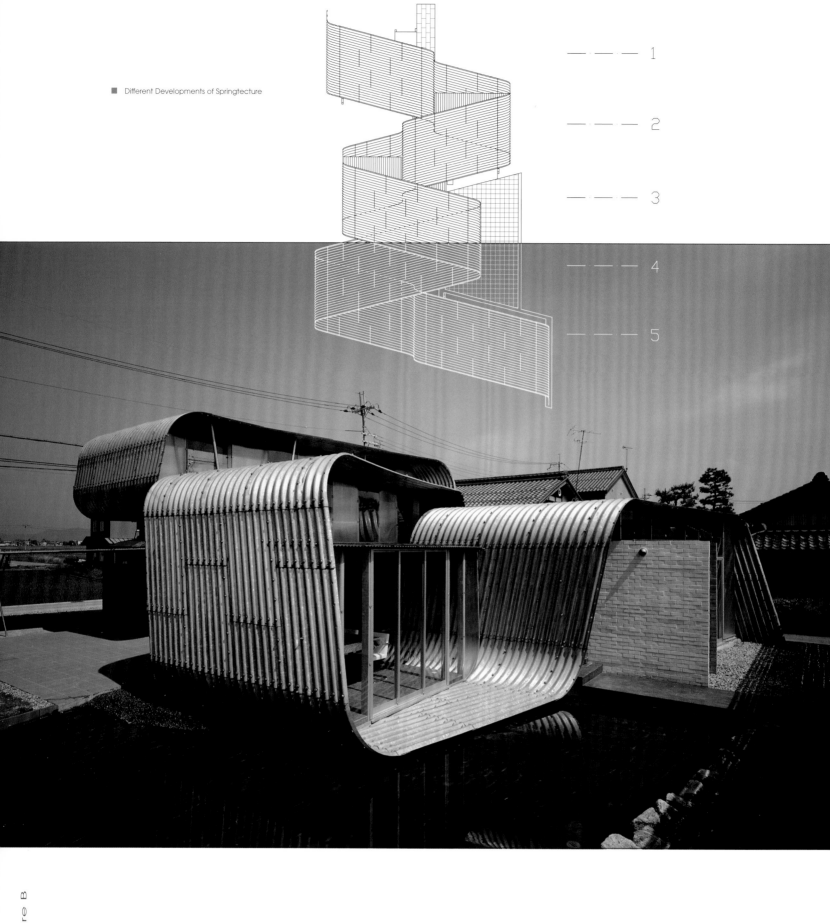

— 2

— 3

— 4

— 5

2

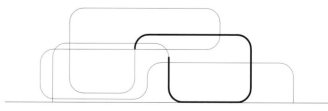

3

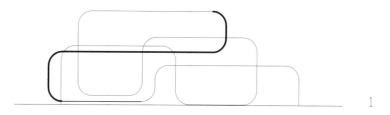

1

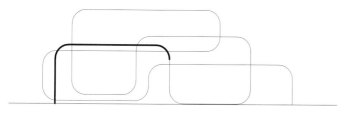

4

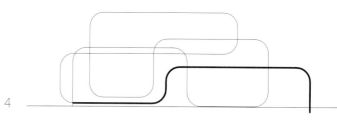

5

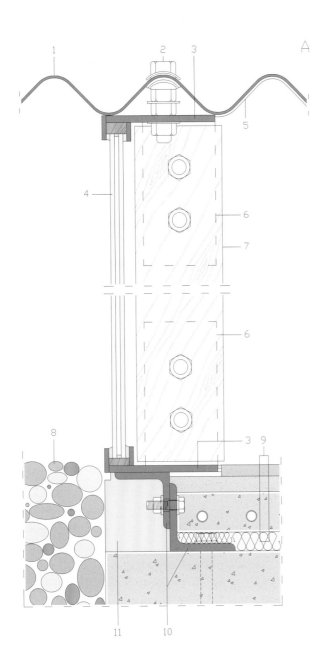

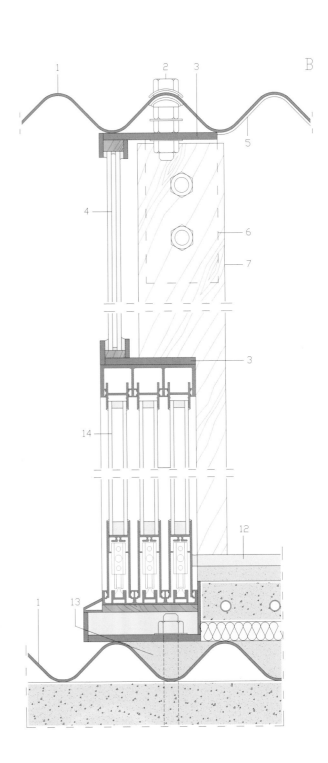

**DETAILS A AND B: GLAZED FAÇADES
VERTICAL SECTIONS – SCALE 1:5**

1. 1/8" (3 mm) thick
   corrugated sheet steel
2. Join between roofing and façade
   mullion using nuts and bolts
3. 3/8" (9 mm) thick steel plate
4. 1/4" (6 mm) thick window
   with insulating glass and
   steel plate frame
5. Heat insulating
   amorphous silicon paint
6. Connecting 1/2" (12 mm)
   steel plate
7. Japanese cyprus façade mullion
8. Ballast

9. 5/8" (15 mm) marble flooring,
   3/4" (20 mm) bedding mortar,
   2 1/8" (54 mm) screed with
   radiant heating system,
   1" (25 mm) board insulation
10. 3 x 3" (75 x 75 mm) and
    3 1/2 x 3 1/2" (90 x 90 mm)
    steel angle profile
11. System connecting glazed
    façade to slab
12. Resin mortar
13. 5/8" (15 mm) thick
    granite flooring
14. Levelling mortar
15. Glazed façade comprising
    three sliding aluminium
    frames and double glazing

The Chesa Futura apartment block in the Engadine Valley fuses state-of-the-art computer design tools and traditional, indigenous building techniques to create an environmentally sensitive structure. Although its form is novel, it utilizes timber construction – one of the oldest, most environmentally benign and sustainable forms of building.

The building consists of three storeys of apartments and two underground levels for car parking. Its bubble-like form is a response to the site and local weather conditions. The site is located on the edge of a slope, looking down over the village towards a lake. The building is lifted above the ground on eight pilotis to ensure that all three storeys benefit from the views of the Engadine Valley and the lake of St Moritz. Raised buildings have a long architectural tradition in Switzerland, where snow lies on the ground for many months of the year. Each floor has been widened to achieve the desired overall floor area, because there is a height restriction on the site and the ground level is not being utilized. To avoid a bulky appearance and in order to maintain views up and down the slope under and around the building, its form has been softened into curves.

The form has been refined using a specially written computer program that has fused the building's plan and section to create a three-dimensional volume. The digital information can also be directly exported to cutting tools to build physical models and ultimately to the machines that will make the timber building components.

In Switzerland, building in timber makes environmental sense for a number of reasons. It reflects local architectural traditions, and it contributes to the established ecology of felling older trees to facilitate forest regeneration.

The frame is constructed from glue-laminated timber beams – consisting of thin sections of wood glued together – in pre-assembled panels of 20 – 23 Ft (6 – 7 m) in length. A steel undercarriage supports the timber frame. The larch shingles that make up the building's skin will respond to weather, change colour over time, and appear as an organic part of the landscape. They are cut by hand by a family that has practised the craft for generations. The shingles were cut from trees at the same altitude as the construction site during the winter when the wood is dry, contains no sap and so will not shrink. The roof is made from copper, a traditional local material sufficiently malleable to be formed on site when temperatures drop well below freezing.

The curved form allows windows to wrap around the façade, providing panoramic views of the lake and surrounding mountains. The building has balconies to the south which benefit from sunlight. It is closed at the back facing the mountains and the coldest weather, providing insulation through its thermal mass.

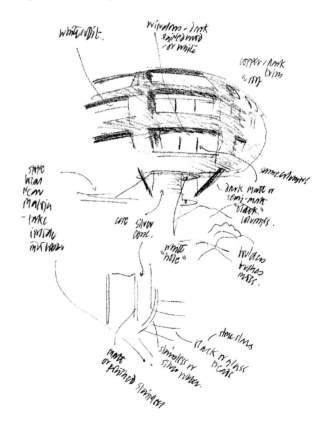

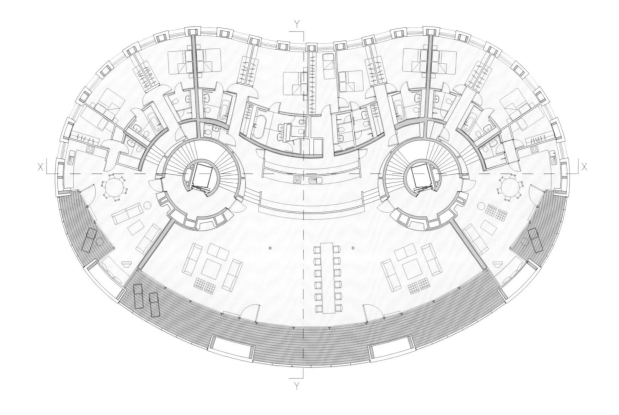

■ Second Floor Plan – Scale 1:300

■ Roof Plan – Scale 1:300

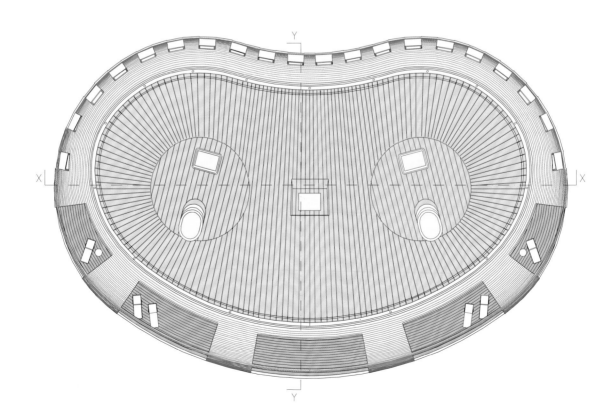

■ North Elevation – Scale 1:300

■ South Elevation – Scale 1:300

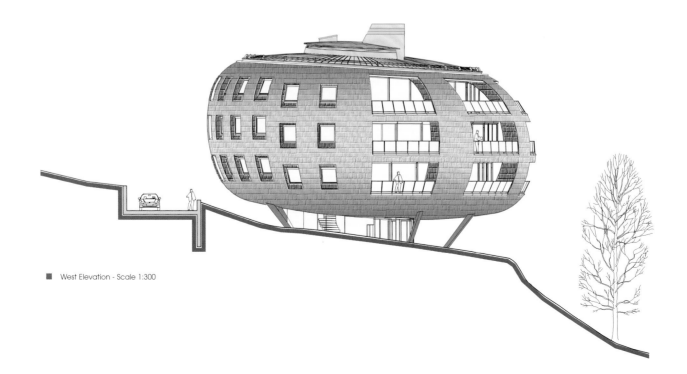

■ West Elevation – Scale 1:300

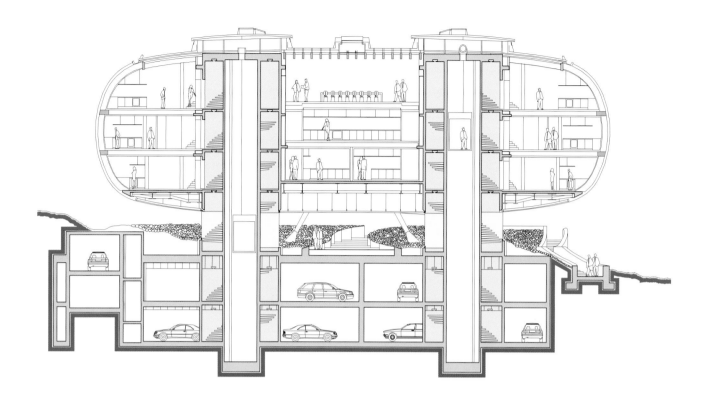

■ XX Section – Scale 1:300

■ YY Section – Scale 1:300

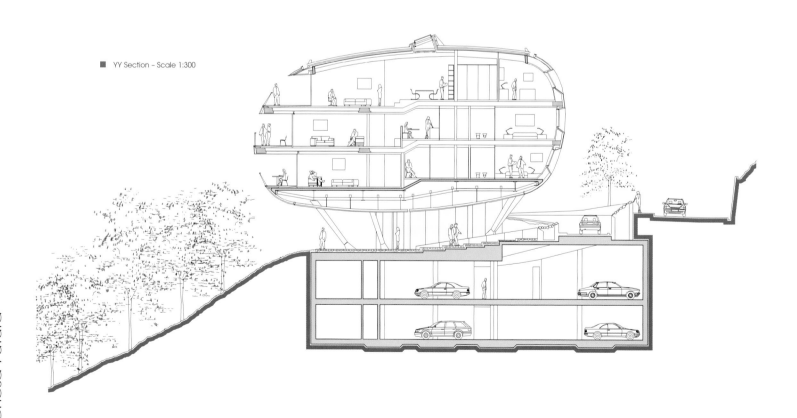

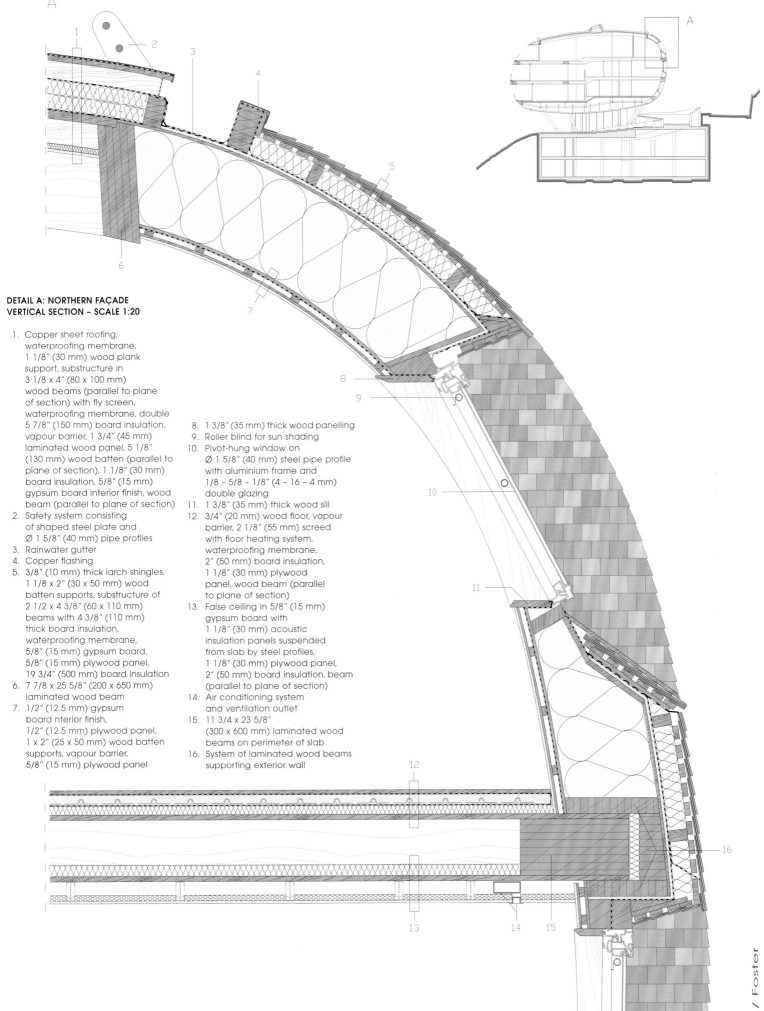

DETAIL A: NORTHERN FAÇADE
VERTICAL SECTION – SCALE 1:20

1. Copper sheet roofing,
   waterproofing membrane,
   1 1/8" (30 mm) wood plank
   support, substructure in
   3 1/8 x 4" (80 x 100 mm)
   wood beams (parallel to plane
   of section) with fly screen,
   waterproofing membrane, double
   5 7/8" (150 mm) board insulation,
   vapour barrier, 1 3/4" (45 mm)
   laminated wood panel, 5 1/8"
   (130 mm) wood batten (parallel to
   plane of section), 1 1/8" (30 mm)
   board insulation, 5/8" (15 mm)
   gypsum board interior finish, wood
   beam (parallel to plane of section)
2. Safety system consisting
   of shaped steel plate and
   Ø 1 5/8" (40 mm) pipe profiles
3. Rainwater gutter
4. Copper flashing
5. 3/8" (10 mm) thick larch shingles,
   1 1/8 x 2" (30 x 50 mm) wood
   batten supports, substructure of
   2 1/2 x 4 3/8" (60 x 110 mm)
   beams with 4 3/8" (110 mm)
   thick board insulation,
   waterproofing membrane,
   5/8" (15 mm) gypsum board,
   5/8" (15 mm) plywood panel,
   19 3/4" (500 mm) board insulation
6. 7 7/8 x 25 5/8" (200 x 650 mm)
   laminated wood beam
7. 1/2" (12.5 mm) gypsum
   board nterior finish,
   1/2" (12.5 mm) plywood panel,
   1 x 2" (25 x 50 mm) wood batten
   supports, vapour barrier,
   5/8" (15 mm) plywood panel

8. 1 3/8" (35 mm) thick wood panelling
9. Roller blind for sun shading
10. Pivot-hung window on
    Ø 1 5/8" (40 mm) steel pipe profile
    with aluminium frame and
    1/8 – 5/8 – 1/8" (4 – 16 – 4 mm)
    double glazing
11. 1 3/8" (35 mm) thick wood sill
12. 3/4" (20 mm) wood floor, vapour
    barrier, 2 1/8" (55 mm) screed
    with floor heating system,
    waterproofing membrane,
    2" (50 mm) board insulation,
    1 1/8" (30 mm) plywood
    panel, wood beam (parallel
    to plane of section)
13. False ceiling in 5/8" (15 mm)
    gypsum board with
    1 1/8" (30 mm) acoustic
    insulation panels suspended
    from slab by steel profiles,
    1 1/8" (30 mm) plywood panel,
    2" (50 mm) board insulation, beam
    (parallel to plane of section)
14. Air conditioning system
    and ventilation outlet
15. 11 3/4 x 23 5/8"
    (300 x 600 mm) laminated wood
    beams on perimeter of slab
16. System of laminated wood beams
    supporting exterior wall

COMMERCIAL AND RESIDENTIAL COMPLEX
BOHINJSKA BISTRICA, SLOVENIA

OFIS ARHITEKTI

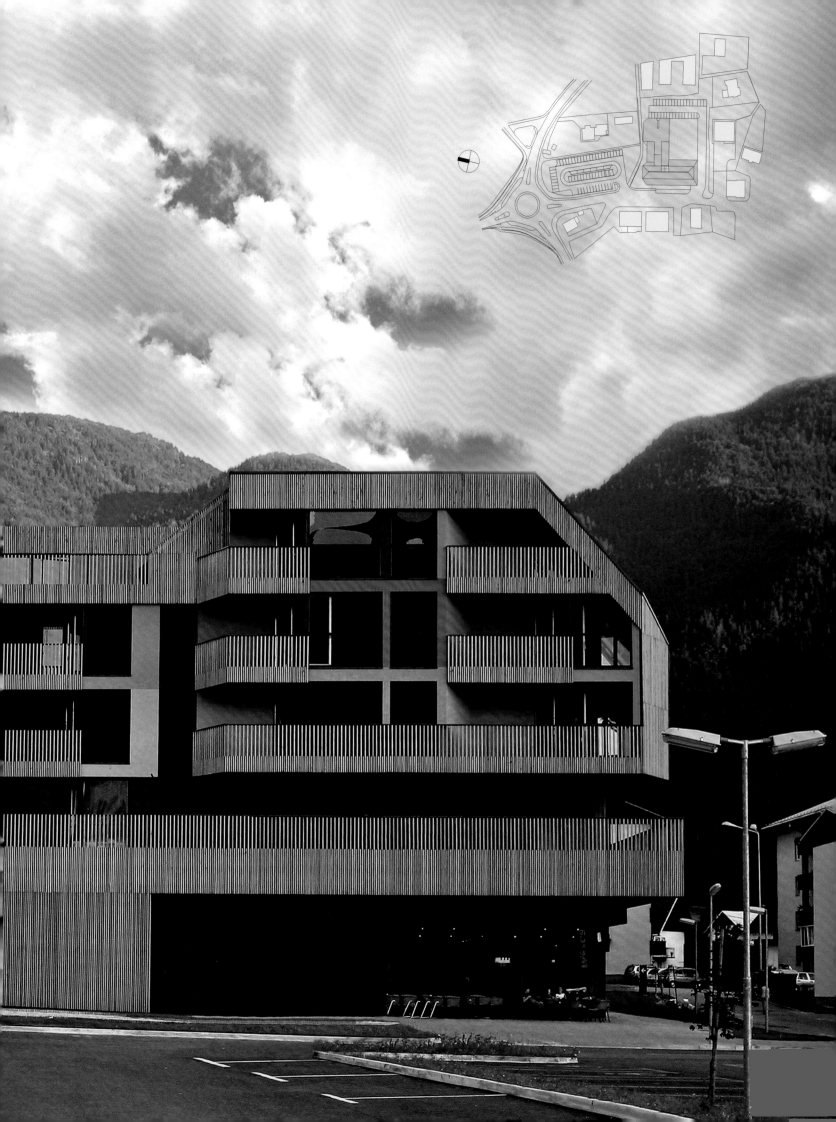

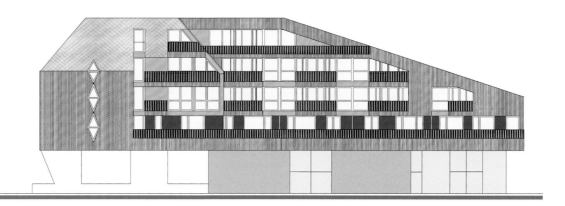

■ South Elevation – Scale 1:400

The shopping centre and residential complex designed by Ofis Arhitekti occupies a central location in the Alpine town of Bohinjska Bistrica near Lake Bohinj, Slovenia. The brief required a new commercial and residential complex where a former shopping centre had once stood.

The two functions are, however, quite separate. A supermarket and a coffee shop occupy the ground floor while the square roof supports a four-storey apartment block and a communal garden for the apartment-dwellers. The recessed ground-floor elevations comprise a characteristic combination of glazing, steel slabs and ample use of larch slat cladding. The steeply sloped roof of the L-shaped residential volume by architects Rok Oman and Špela Videcnik incorporates the last two floors to create attic apartments. The gradient is especially accentuated over the east

elevation, giving the effect of a stepped volume similar to the nearby mountains rising against the sky. This profile also preserves the panoramic views for neighbouring constructions to the north. The apartments on both wings are compact, laid out along a central corridor. Sizes vary from bedsit to three-room apartment.

The more sheltered elevations of the residential volume present as open façades punctuated by linear balconies. This contrasts to the exposed western façade, which is more closed with recessed balconies flush with the outer wall. The façade is clad with a decorative alternation of larch panels and slats, and fibre cement lozenges, these latter also used on the roof. The slender wooden slats forming the balcony and terrace parapets give the whole building a transparent lightness.

First Floor Plan – Scale 1:400

1. Entrance
2. Living room
3. Kitchen
4. Bedroom
5. Study
6. Terrace
7. Garden

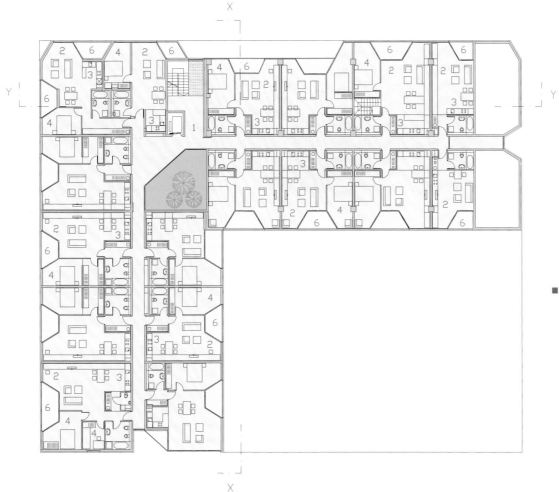

Second Floor Plan – Scale 1:400

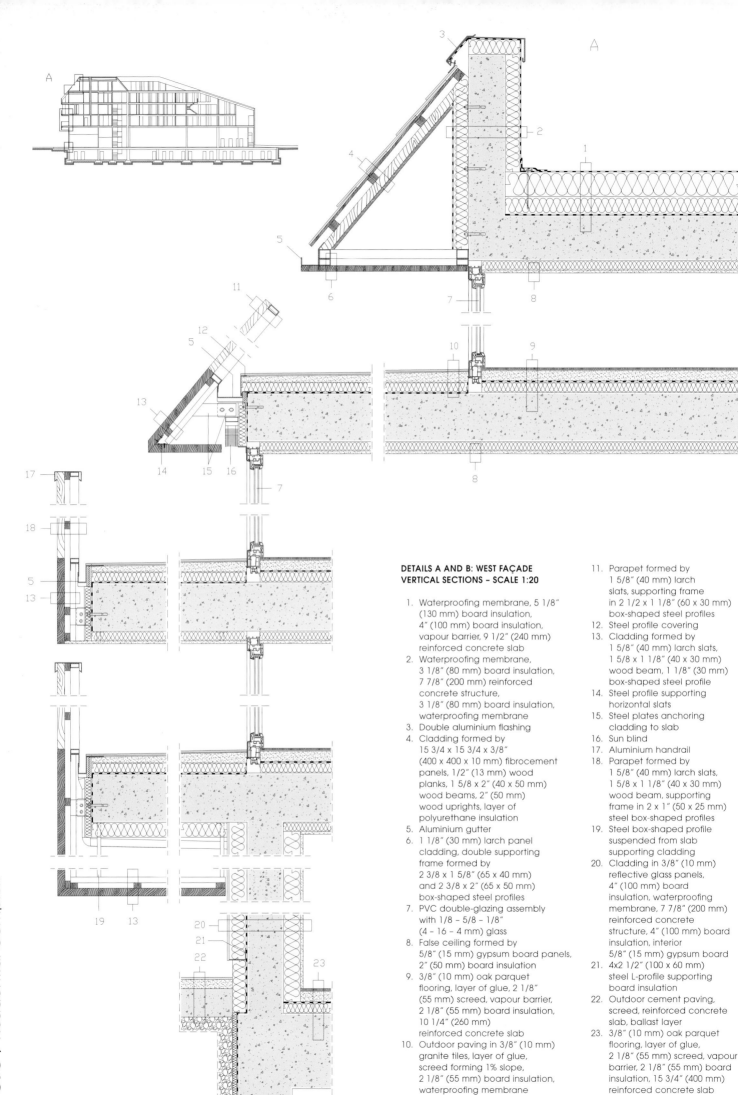

DETAILS A AND B: WEST FAÇADE
VERTICAL SECTIONS – SCALE 1:20

1. Waterproofing membrane, 5 1/8" (130 mm) board insulation, 4" (100 mm) board insulation, vapour barrier, 9 1/2" (240 mm) reinforced concrete slab
2. Waterproofing membrane, 3 1/8" (80 mm) board insulation, 7 7/8" (200 mm) reinforced concrete structure, 3 1/8" (80 mm) board insulation, waterproofing membrane
3. Double aluminium flashing
4. Cladding formed by 15 3/4 x 15 3/4 x 3/8" (400 x 400 x 10 mm) fibrocement panels, 1/2" (13 mm) wood planks, 1 5/8 x 2" (40 x 50 mm) wood beams, 2" (50 mm) wood uprights, layer of polyurethane insulation
5. Aluminium gutter
6. 1 1/8" (30 mm) larch panel cladding, double supporting frame formed by 2 3/8 x 1 5/8" (65 x 40 mm) and 2 3/8 x 2" (65 x 50 mm) box-shaped steel profiles
7. PVC double-glazing assembly with 1/8 – 5/8 – 1/8" (4 – 16 – 4 mm) glass
8. False ceiling formed by 5/8" (15 mm) gypsum board panels, 2" (50 mm) board insulation
9. 3/8" (10 mm) oak parquet flooring, layer of glue, 2 1/8" (55 mm) screed, vapour barrier, 2 1/8" (55 mm) board insulation, 10 1/4" (260 mm) reinforced concrete slab
10. Outdoor paving in 3/8" (10 mm) granite tiles, layer of glue, screed forming 1% slope, 2 1/8" (55 mm) board insulation, waterproofing membrane
11. Parapet formed by 1 5/8" (40 mm) larch slats, supporting frame in 2 1/2 x 1 1/8" (60 x 30 mm) box-shaped steel profiles
12. Steel profile covering
13. Cladding formed by 1 5/8" (40 mm) larch slats, 1 5/8 x 1 1/8" (40 x 30 mm) wood beam, 1 1/8" (30 mm) box-shaped steel profile
14. Steel profile supporting horizontal slats
15. Steel plates anchoring cladding to slab
16. Sun blind
17. Aluminium handrail
18. Parapet formed by 1 5/8" (40 mm) larch slats, 1 5/8 x 1 1/8" (40 x 30 mm) wood beam, supporting frame in 2 x 1" (50 x 25 mm) steel box-shaped profiles
19. Steel box-shaped profile suspended from slab supporting cladding
20. Cladding in 3/8" (10 mm) reflective glass panels, 4" (100 mm) board insulation, waterproofing membrane, 7 7/8" (200 mm) reinforced concrete structure, 4" (100 mm) board insulation, interior 5/8" (15 mm) gypsum board
21. 4x2 1/2" (100 x 60 mm) steel L-profile supporting board insulation
22. Outdoor cement paving, screed, reinforced concrete slab, ballast layer
23. 3/8" (10 mm) oak parquet flooring, layer of glue, 2 1/8" (55 mm) screed, vapour barrier, 2 1/8" (55 mm) board insulation, 15 3/4" (400 mm) reinforced concrete slab

■ XX Section – Scale 1:400

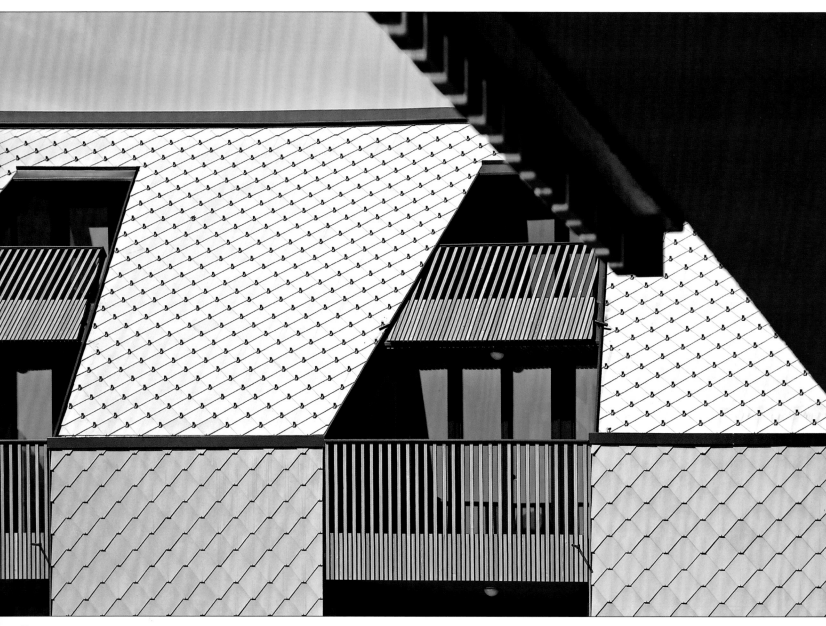

■ West Elevation – Scale 1:400

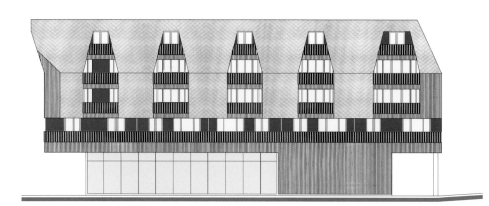

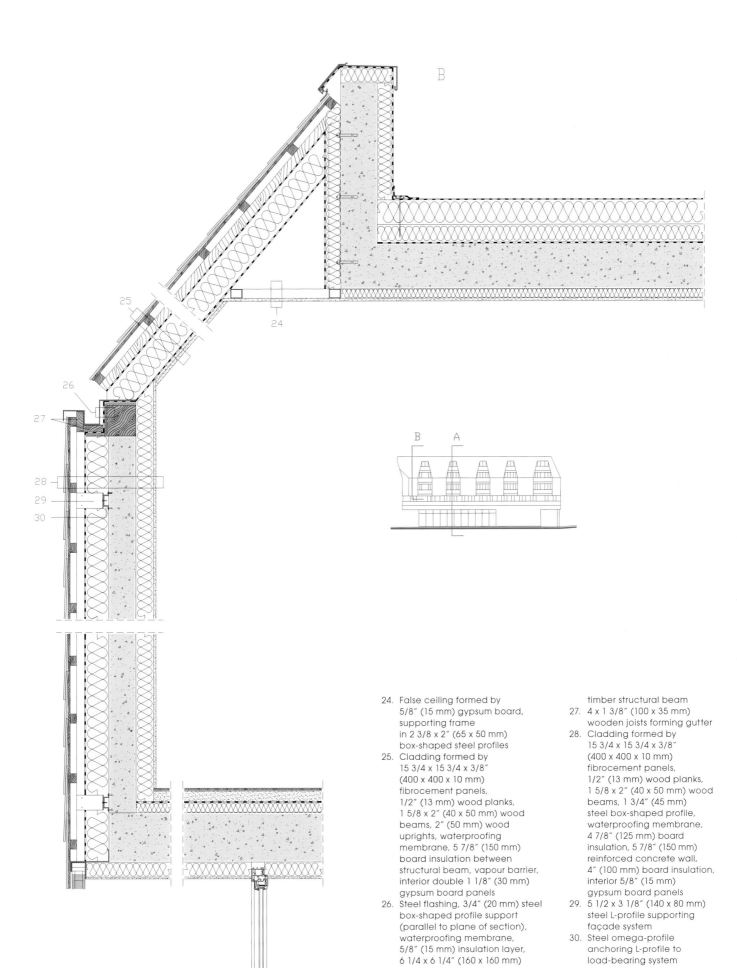

24. False ceiling formed by
    5/8" (15 mm) gypsum board,
    supporting frame
    in 2 3/8 x 2" (65 x 50 mm)
    box-shaped steel profiles
25. Cladding formed by
    15 3/4 x 15 3/4 x 3/8"
    (400 x 400 x 10 mm)
    fibrocement panels,
    1/2" (13 mm) wood planks,
    1 5/8 x 2" (40 x 50 mm) wood
    beams, 2" (50 mm) wood
    uprights, waterproofing
    membrane, 5 7/8" (150 mm)
    board insulation between
    structural beam, vapour barrier,
    interior double 1 1/8" (30 mm)
    gypsum board panels
26. Steel flashing, 3/4" (20 mm) steel
    box-shaped profile support
    (parallel to plane of section),
    waterproofing membrane,
    5/8" (15 mm) insulation layer,
    6 1/4 x 6 1/4" (160 x 160 mm)

    timber structural beam
27. 4 x 1 3/8" (100 x 35 mm)
    wooden joists forming gutter
28. Cladding formed by
    15 3/4 x 15 3/4 x 3/8"
    (400 x 400 x 10 mm)
    fibrocement panels,
    1/2" (13 mm) wood planks,
    1 5/8 x 2" (40 x 50 mm) wood
    beams, 1 3/4" (45 mm)
    steel box-shaped profile,
    waterproofing membrane,
    4 7/8" (125 mm) board
    insulation, 5 7/8" (150 mm)
    reinforced concrete wall,
    4" (100 mm) board insulation,
    interior 5/8" (15 mm)
    gypsum board panels
29. 5 1/2 x 3 1/8" (140 x 80 mm)
    steel L-profile supporting
    façade system
30. Steel omega-profile
    anchoring L-profile to
    load-bearing system

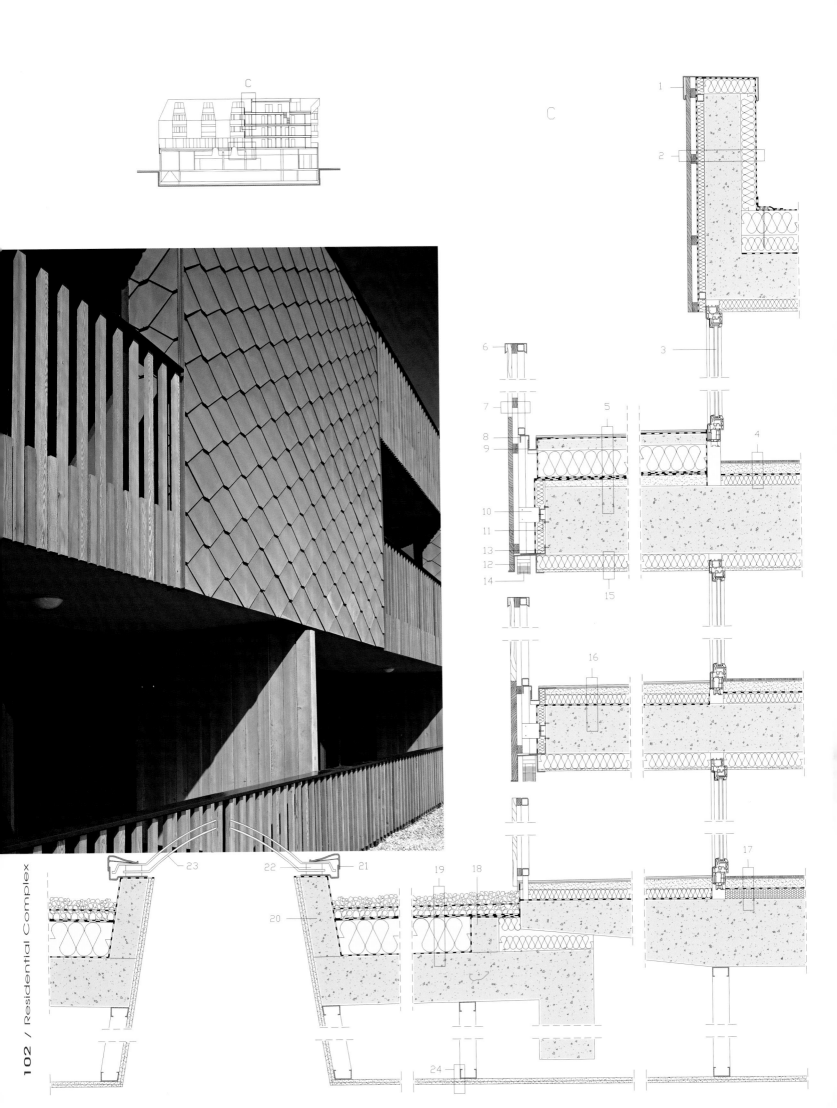

**DETAIL C: SOUTH FAÇADE
AND SHOPPING CENTRE ROOF
VERTICAL SECTION – SCALE 1:20**

1. Aluminium flashing
2. Cladding formed by 1" (25 mm) larch slats, wood supporting beams, waterproofing membrane, board insulation inside frame of 1 5/8 x 1 5/8" (40 x 40 mm) steel box-shaped profiles,

7 7/8" (200 mm) reinforced concrete structure, 3 1/8" (80 mm) board insulation, waterproofing membrane
3. PVC double-glazing assembly with 1/8 – 5/8 – 1/8" (4 – 16 – 4 mm) glass
4. 3/8" (10 mm) oak parquet flooring, layer of glue, 2 1/8" (55 mm) screed, vapour barrier, 2 1/8" (55 mm) board insulation
5. Outdoor paving in 3/8"

(10 mm) granite tiles, layer of glue, waterproofing membrane, 2 1/2" (60 mm) reinforced concrete slab, 5 1/2" (140 mm) board insulation, non-woven membrane, waterproofing membrane, non-woven membrane, screed forming 1.5% slope, 14 1/8" (360 mm) reinforced concrete slab
6. Aluminium handrail

7. Parapet formed by 1" (25 mm) larch slats, 2 x 1 1/8" (50 x 30 mm) wood beam, supporting frame in 1 5/8 x 1 5/8" (40 x 40 mm) steel box-shaped profiles
8. Steel profile anchoring gutter to box-shaped profile
9. Gutter
10. Steel L-profile supporting façade system
11. Steel omega-profile anchoring

L-profile to load-bearing system
12. Steel profile covering supporting sun blind
13. Steel L-profile anchoring profile to slab
14. Sun blind
15. 5/8" (15 mm) gypsum board panel, 3 1/8" (80 mm) board insulation
16. Outdoor paving in 3/8" (10 mm) granite tiles, layer of

glue, screed forming 1% slope, 2 1/8" (55 mm) board insulation, waterproofing membrane, 10 1/4" (260 mm) reinforced concrete slab
17. 3/8" (10 mm) oak parquet flooring, layer of glue, 2 1/8" (55 mm) screed, vapour barrier, 2 1/8" (55 mm) acoustic board insulation, reinforced concrete slab

18. Reinforced concrete edging
19. Gravel paving, non-woven membrane, 2" (50 mm) ballast drainage layer, double waterproofing membrane, 7 1/8" (180 mm) board insulation, vapour barrier, 10 1/4" (260 mm) reinforced concrete slab
20. Reinforced concrete edging supporting skylight

21. System securing skylight to edging
22. Neoprene seal
23. Plexiglas skylight
24. False ceiling formed by double 1 1/8" (30 mm) gypsum board panels, supporting frame of steel C-profiles anchored to slab

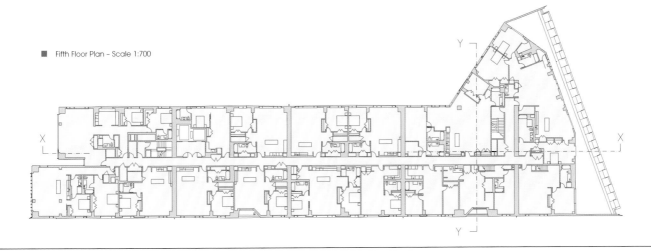

The Macallen building, the first large project to be completed by Office dA, slopes up to the border of South Boston as a sleek monolith. According to Nader Tehrani, who directs Office dA with Monica Ponce de Leon, this enigmatic character may even allude to the Sphinx of ancient Egypt. Given its exposure – a post-industrial site with raised highway and bus garage to the south, and multiple railway tracks to the west – and its contents – 140 apartments, parking, retail spaces – the building is inevitably monumental. Yet its skin or pelt, adjusting in turn to each exposure, and its incised ridge of private terraces suggest a quality that is almost animalistic.

The massing results from the union or hybridization of two standard forms – row housing and the point tower. The new structure rises and stretches along heavily trafficked West Fourth Street to a peak fourteen storeys high (eleven storeys of apartments above three trays of parking). The short lower end and this long inhabited wall together protect a raised communal terrace facing west and north. The observant will notice particular qualities to the skin on all façades. The walls are not of course load-bearing – they are taut membranes made from brick, glass and metal panel. Vertical panels of brick create an elegant chequerboard pattern of positive and negative, the "negative" simulating the scale and appearance of normative window openings. The intermittent glazed panes are progressively recessed from this outer brick datum such that light, reflections and shadow result in a complex, shallow whole.

Office dA's reputation is in part due to its critical exploration of materiality, the way surfaces meet, and the effects generated by surface manipulation. The tallest façade, to the west and soaring above the garage entrance, is dressed in a taut scrim of corrugated aluminium. Pedestrian access is from Macallen Way to the north, into a foyer inlaid with black artificial stone. To either side of the slim entrance canopy, the garage is screened by wafer-like aluminium fins that act as geometric camouflage. The terrace above can be accessed from a splayed, open-air staircase from Dorchester Avenue. This palette of elements is installed within very narrow bands of space, a composite epidermis wrapping the vertical boundaries of the project. Although taut and shallow, both long façades offer clues to the unusual structure organizing the bulk of

the building. It's a system of staggered trusses invented by, and named after, the distinguished Boston engineer William LeMessurier. Spanning between the long elevations, the trusses allow for circulation within the building in both longitudinal and transverse directions, for ease of car access and apartment layout respectively. Their outer edges are capped by exposed metal covers which give rhythm to the north and south façades.

These protruding elements stagger across the walls of taut bronzed aluminium, skipping levels to align vertically every second storey, and suggest knuckles or pins in the great metal planes of the façades. The elevations are lined in horizontal strata – reminiscent of film strips or a music score – which corral all fenestration, are occasionally punctured by recessed terraces, and also fold back very slightly so that the entire façade appears to ripple in sunlight. The window units shift position within these bands depending on the arrangement of apartments behind. The trusses are pierced only by the long central corridor on each floor. Most apartments are single-storey units that can, if desired, be joined laterally. Beneath the angled roof, however, are double- and triple-storey apartments with internal staircases and the splayed rooftop terraces. In two irregular yet spacious units, at the juncture of the monolith along West Fourth Street and the lower segment on Dorchester Avenue, trusses are exposed as walk-through, floor-to-ceiling elements.

If the practice's work is characterized by a pragmatic sensuosity, evidenced here by the stone planes and stainless steel screen of the entry foyer, the Macallen building has also embraced the environmental agenda. In fact, it is aiming for a Gold LEED rating. This can be partially achieved through the material selection: recycled cotton wall insulation, grass cloth on corridor walls, bamboo flooring, reconstituted Macassar ebony or zebra wood veneers, and quartz aggregate work tops. In addition, the patterned sedum roof provides insulation, produces oxygen, and recycles storm water run-off.

At the Macallen building, the Office dA team has finessed practical concerns and conceptual interests to realize an architecture that is useful, complex and urban.

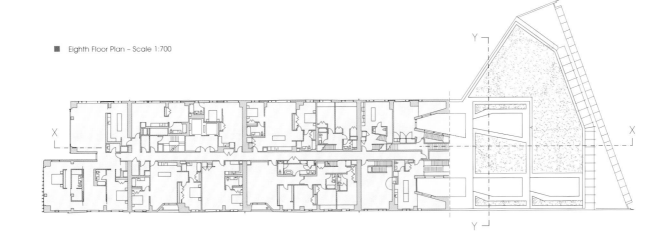

■ Eighth Floor Plan – Scale 1:700

■ Site Plan – Not to Scale

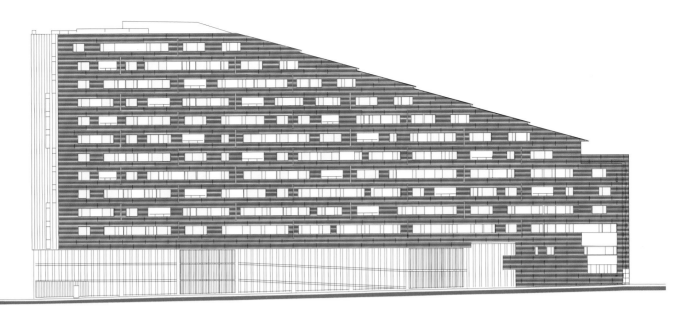

■ South Elevation – Scale 1:700

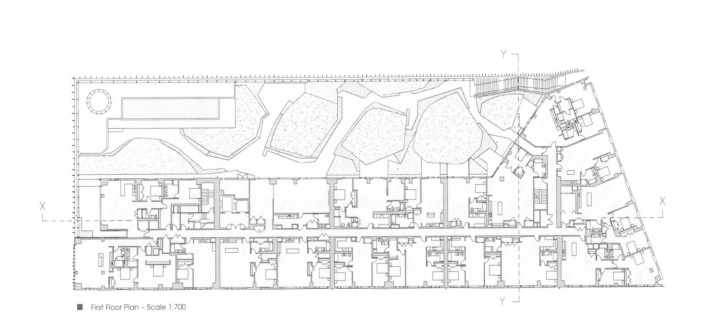

■ First Floor Plan – Scale 1:700

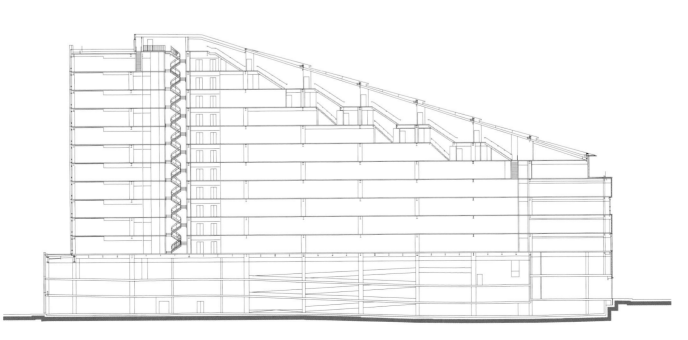

■ XX Longitudinal Section – Scale 1:700

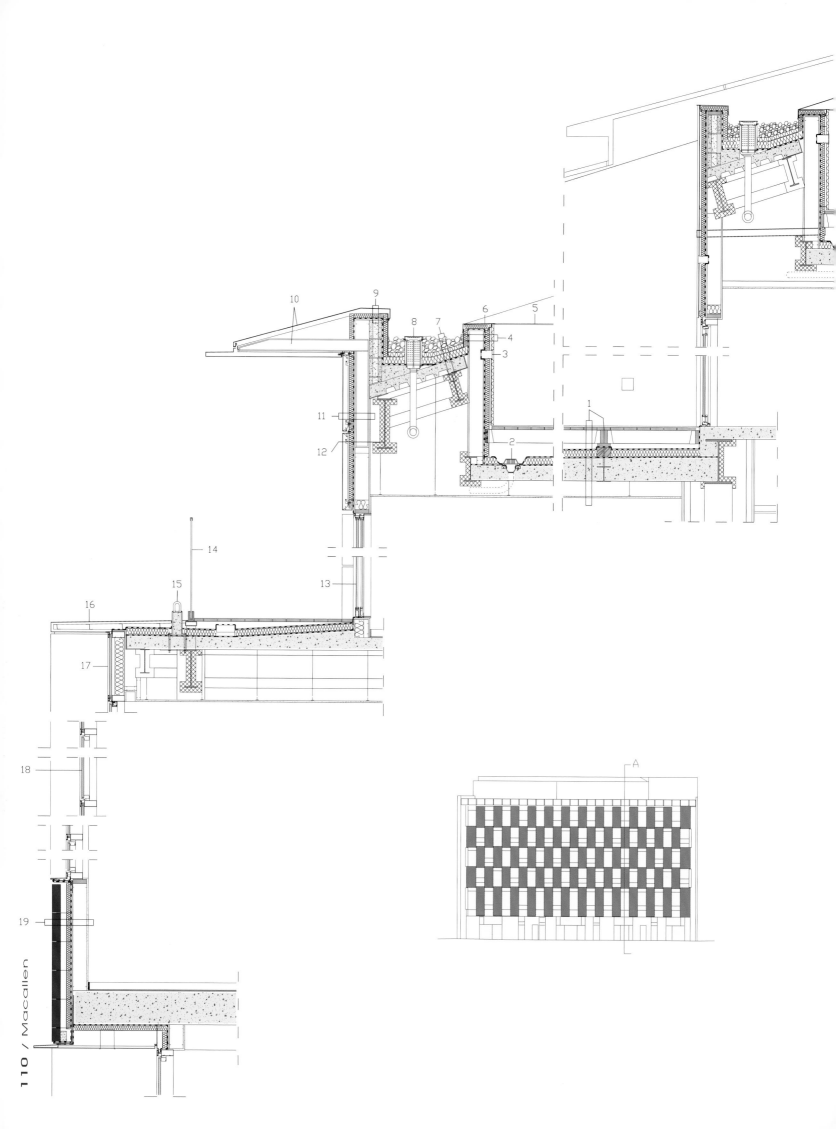

DETAIL A: EAST FAÇADE
VERTICAL SECTION - SCALE 1:40

1. IPE timber plank decking, timber joist frame supported by horizontal timber members nailed to double T-section steel beams H 6 1/4" (160 mm), air space, PVC waterproofing membrane, 2 3/4" (70 mm) rigid insulating layer, moisture trap, sloping reinforced concrete slab for water drainage,

5/8" (15 mm) painted gypsum board suspended ceiling, supported by tie-rods suspended from slab
2. Rainwater drainage ditch on terrace, covered with perforated lid
3. Recessed outdoor wall lighting unit
4. Corrugated aluminium panels supported by Z-profiles, 1" (25 mm) air space, 1 3/4" (45 mm) rigid insulating panel, waterproofing membrane, 5/8" (16 mm) high-density fibreglass

panel, waterproofing membrane, frame in 5 7/8" (150 mm) steel C-profiles, 5/8" (16 mm) high-density fibreglass panel, waterproofing membrane, 1 3/4" (45 mm) rigid insulating panel, aluminium closure sheet
5. Aluminium angular profile separating vertical and horizontal sheets, aligned with angular profile welded to flashing
6. Aluminium flashing
7. Ballast layer, 1 5/8" (40 mm) corrugated drainage panel,

2 3/4" (70 mm) insulation layer, waterproofing membrane, 5 1/8" (130 mm) composite slab consisting of lightweight concrete fill over corrugated sheeting, steel closure L-plate, 12 1/4" (310 mm) H double T-section steel beam lined with fireproofing insulation
8. Rainwater drainage ditch opening lined with perforated membrane covered with bronze grating and fitted with low closure device in water-repellent putty

9. Aluminium flashing, 2" (50 mm) rigid insulating layer, waterproofing membrane, 5/8" (16 mm) high-density fibreglass panel, concrete blocks with 5 1/2" (140 mm) cement mortar core
10. Painted steel closure panels hooked to galvanized steel bracket attached to steel wall frame
11. 2 1/2" (60 mm) water-repellent aluminium box panel lining with 2" (50 mm) rigid insulating

core, moisture trap, 5/8" (16 mm) high-density fibreglass panel, frame in 5 7/8" (150 mm) steel C-profiles
12. 20 1/2" (520 mm) H steel double T-section spandrel with fireproofing layer
13. Sliding door in 1/4 – 1/2 – 1/4" (6 – 12 – 6 mm) thermal insulating glass with champagne-coloured aluminium frame
14. Parapet in tempered plate glass 1/2" (12 mm) thick

on aluminium frame
15. Steel support hooks on concrete base for securing window-cleaning system
16. Bracket frame in steel Z-profiles lined with steel panels to support window cleaning system
17. Fixed mat panel with 1/4 – 1/2 – 1/4" (6 – 12 – 6 mm) double glazing, champagne-coloured aluminium support frame, 4" (100 mm) insulating layer

18. Profile system on aluminium frame with 1/4 – 1/2 – 1/4" (6 – 12 – 6 mm) double glazing
19. 3 1/2" (90 mm) brick cladding joined with steel hoops, 2 3/4" (70 mm) air space, 2" (50 mm) rigid insulating panel, moisture trap, 5/8" (16 mm) high-density fibreglass panel, 5 7/8" (150 mm) steel C-profiles frame, 5/8" (15 mm) gypsum board panel

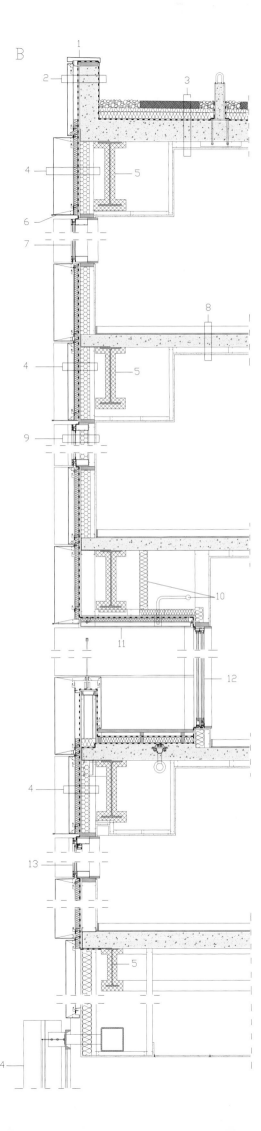

DETAIL B: SOUTH FAÇADE
VERTICAL SECTION – SCALE 1:40

1. Aluminium closure flashing
2. Alcoa sheet aluminium cladding with braided finish and 2 3/4" (70 mm) steel supports, 2" (50 mm) air space, waterproofing membrane, 5/8" (16 mm) fibreglass panel, 7 7/8" (200 mm) reinforced concrete closing wall, waterproofing membrane, painted aluminium sheeting
3. Green roof, 1 5/8" (40 mm) corrugated drainage panel, 3" (75 mm) rigid insulating panel, waterproofing membrane, 8 5/8" (220 mm) reinforced concrete floor, 5/8" (16 mm) gypsum board suspended ceiling on frame in 2 1/8" (55 mm) steel C-profiles
4. Variable thickness cladding in Alcoa aluminium box sheeting with braided finish and steel supports, 2" (50 mm) rigid insulating panel, moisture trap, 5/8" (16 mm) high-density fibreglass panel, 3 1/8" (80 mm) sound insulation layer sandwiched in frame with steel C-profiles
5. Steel double T-section beam H 26 3/4" (680 mm) lined with fireproofing layer
6. Aluminium separation plate, sealed with extruded silicone

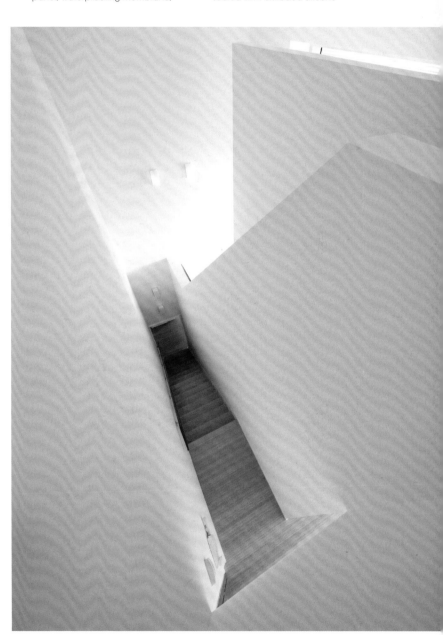

7. Glass wall fixed to aluminium frame and 1/4 – 1/2 – 1/4" (6 – 12 – 6 mm) double glazing and timber internal glazing bar
8. 3" (75 mm) timber skirting board, 1/2" (12 mm) timber parquetry floor, 5 3/8" (135 mm) reinforced concrete floor slab, suspended ceiling in gypsum board panels supported by steel C-profiles fastened to floor slab
9. 1" (25 mm) white painted corrugated aluminium panel on frame in steel box-shaped profiles, 3 1/8" (80 mm) sound insulation layer, frame with 2 1/2" (60 mm) C-profiles, 5/8" (15 mm) gypsum board panel
10. Sprinkler system recessed in suspended ceiling with thermally insulated water delivery pipe
11. Suspended ceiling of balcony lined with brown aluminium panels
12. Sliding door in 1/4 – 1/2 – 1/4" (6 – 12 – 6 mm) thermal insulating glass with champagne-coloured aluminium frame
13. Aluminium window frame with 1/4 – 1/2 – 1/4" (6 – 12 – 6 mm) double glazing
14. Frame with steel box-shaped profiles and steel rod grating closing the garage level

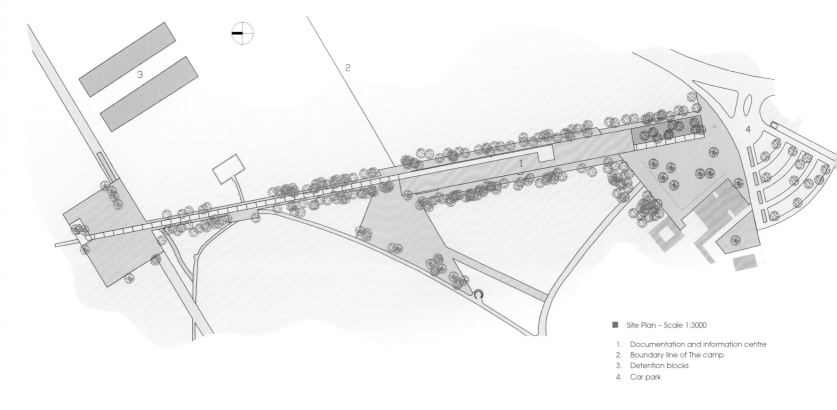

The brief for the new information and documentation centre at Bergen-Belsen, a former Nazi concentration and prisoner of war camp, was put out to competition in 2003. The winning entry by architects Engel and Zimmermann is a monolithic monument in the form of a fairly slender, two-storey block, 656 Ft (200 m) long and 59 Ft (18 m) wide.

Located along the edges of the former camp, of which only few traces remain, the building's layout is rigorously functional. It stands like a walk-through sculpture reaching out into the Heidewald forest. The architecture is radical and direct, its emotional impact strong. The solid volume is pierced only by niches and lights with minimalist frames. The stark geometry, essential materials (unrendered concrete and glass), neutral colours and total absence of any form of decoration reinforce the building's imposing physical presence. The pure lines create an aura of silence. There is an abstract tension in the forms and materials that tangibly evoke the terror that reigned at this scene of unspeakable crimes against humanity. The architectural programme is a vibrant statement of how a place of remembrance of past suffering can be coupled to the function of providing a historical documentation centre of Nazism.

The building has been sited where the old road linking Celle to Hörste once ran before the concentration camp changed the landscape. The

entrance – laden with symbolism and emotional charge – seems carved out of the solid, unrendered concrete wall.

The complex comprises two separate units: a reception, information and services area and, immediately behind, the exhibition space proper. The cantilevered volume of the entrance is the starting point for two separate circulation routes. The first takes visitors into the building, rising almost imperceptibly as it progresses through the exhibition areas. These are set out on three levels reflecting the type of information provided: basic information; more detailed enquiry into the victims of Nazi barbarity, and the wider historical and political context for what happened in the concentration camp. At the far end of the long exhibition hall, a wide ribbon window gives on to the exterior – significantly the boundary of the former camp. At this point the building is slightly raised from the ground, hovering in permanent tension as if paying silent homage to the place. The exhibition continues on the first floor, which also houses the library and archive holding original documents of the period.

The second – external – circulation route has been aptly named the "stony path". Enclosed between the building and a high wall, the path runs parallel to the exhibition rooms the whole length of the building, an unroofed corridor leading to the other areas of the camp, all of which are enclosed by sheer concrete walls.

■ Ground Floor Plan – Scale 1:500

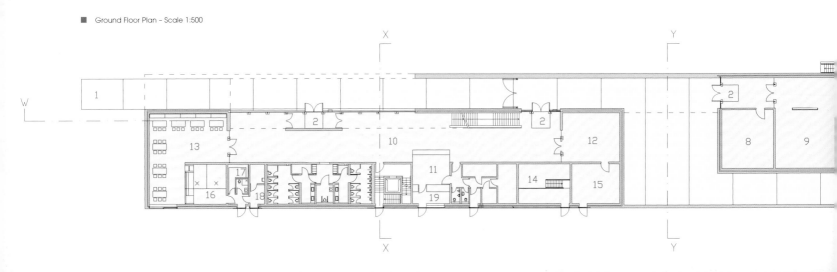

3   4   5   7

6

1

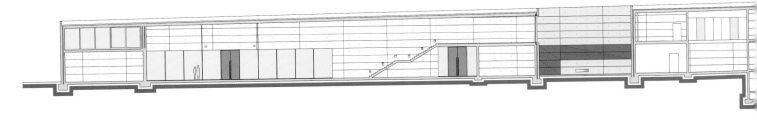

■ WW Section – Scale 1:500

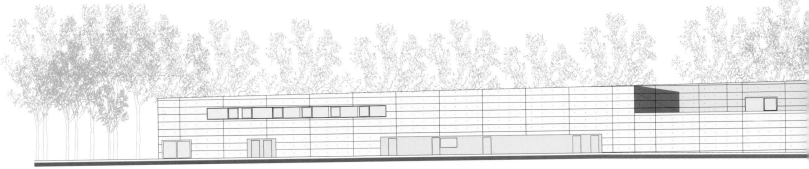

■ East Elevation – Scale 1:500

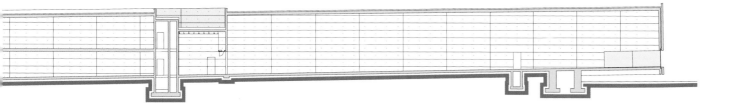

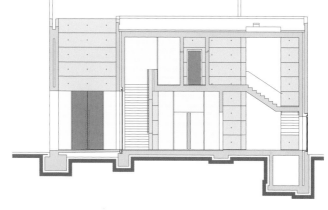

1. Pathway to entrance
2. Entrance
3. Prisoner-of-war camp exhibition
4. Video show room
5. Exhibition cabinets
6. Concentration camp exhibition
7. Historical and
   topographical documentation
8. Storage room
9. Exhibition prologue
10. Foyer
11. Information desk
12. Bookshop
13. Cafeteria
14. Plant and services
15. Book storage
16. Kitchen
17. Food storage
18. Waste storage
19. First-aid station

■ XX Section – Scale 1:250

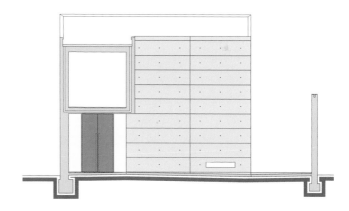

■ YY Section – Scale 1:250

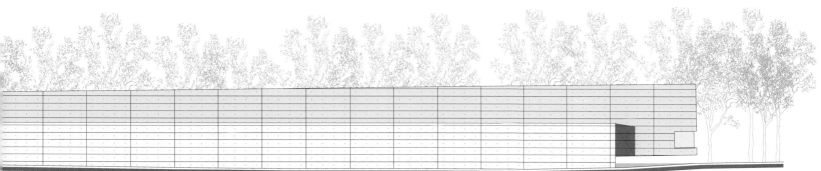

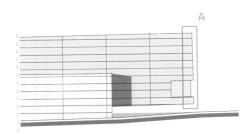

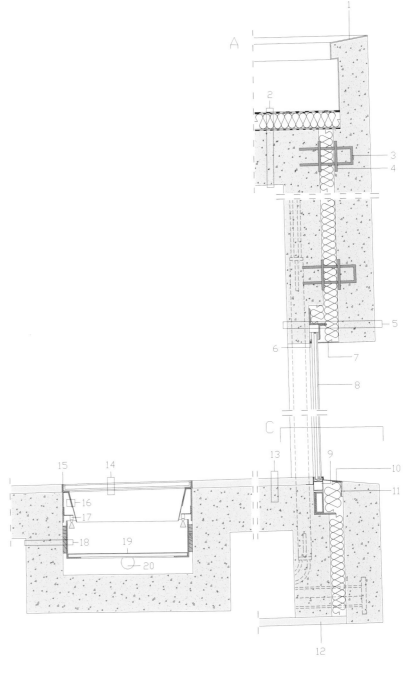

DETAILS A, B AND C:
NORTHERN FAÇADE PROJECTING
VOLUME – VERTICAL AND
HORIZONTAL SECTIONS – SCALE 1:25

1. Layer of transparent
impregnating waterproofing
with mat finish protecting roof
2. Waterproofing membrane,
3 1/8 x 9 1/2 (80 x 240 mm)
insulation on ≥ 2% slope,
screed, vapour barrier,
14 1/8" (360 mm) reinforced
concrete slab with

exposed concrete
3. 1 1/8" (27 mm) Ø steel tie
between two reinforced
concrete structures
4. Tie anchoring plate
5. 9 7/8" (250 mm) reinforced
concrete structure with
exposed concrete, 4 + 4"
(100 + 100 mm) board insulation,
system for fixing strap
window consisting of
4 3/8 x 4 3/8 x 3/8"
(110 x 110 x 10 mm) steel profile
fixed with anchors and screwed

to 4 3/8 x 2 x 5/16" (110 x 50 x 8 mm)
steel profile, 5 7/8" (150 mm)
steel window mullion
set in reinforced
concrete structure
6. Silicone seal, lead fill, continuous
joint in UV-resistant black silicone
7. 3/16" (5 mm) thick
sheet steel cover
8. Strip window with
5/16 – 5/8 – 5/16 + 5/16"
(8 – 16 – 8 + 8 mm) double
glazing fixed at end
9. Frame in 2 3/8 x 2 1/2"

(65 x 60 mm) box-shaped
aluminium profiles for
ventilation and removal
of condensation
10. 1/8" (3 mm) sheet
steel on 6° slope
11. Steel L-profile fastening
sheet steel
12. Concrete floor 2" (50 mm),
11 3/4" (300 mm)
reinforced concrete slab
13. Walkable glazed area in
5/16" (8 mm) scratch-resistant
security glass, 1" (25 mm) airspace,

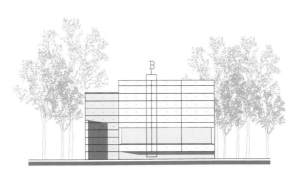

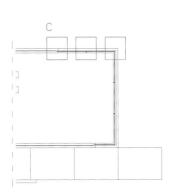

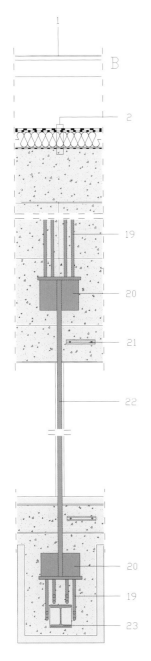

13. 3/8" (10 mm) sealed glass panel with back silicone seals
14. 5/16" (8 mm) shaped galvanized steel plate bolted to reinforced concrete slab
15. Casing in 1/8" (3 mm) steel on 3/16" (5 mm) steel profile screwed to shaped galvanized steel plate
16. Fluorescent tube lighting
17. 1" (25 mm) platform with 1/16" (2 mm) steel surface
18. 3 1/2" (90 mm) Ø cabling hole
19. 3/4" (20 mm) Ø anchor rods

20. 4 5/8 x 7 7/8 x 3/4" (120 x 200 x 20 mm) steel plates joined to form T
21. 1 1/8 x 7 7/8" (30 x 200 mm) horizontal system of glass fasteners
22. 1 1/8 x 3 1/2" (30 x 90 mm) steel window mullion
23. 5 1/2 x 5 1/2" (140 x 140 mm) I-beam supporting projecting volume
24. Ventilation grille

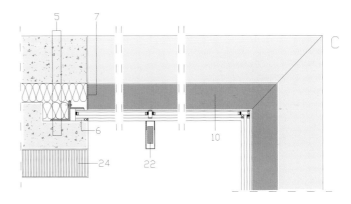

■ Ground Floor Plan - Scale 1:600

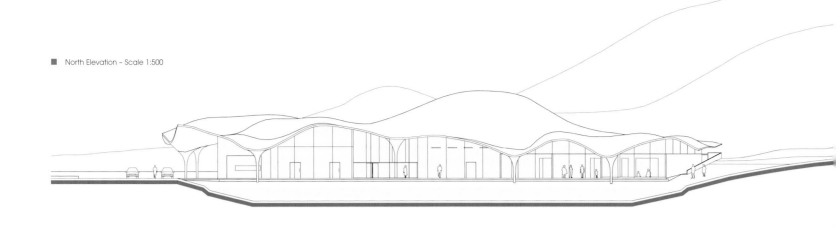

Going beyond Modernism, creating "living" spaces that impart emotions, eschewing the soulless box-like buildings of modern-day consumerism. This, for Toyo Ito, is what "New 'Real' in architecture" is all about. This was also the title of his itinerant exhibition shown at the Hayama Museum of Modern Art, in 2007, a show that looked closely at how a creative idea turns into a realized project. Parts of buildings in real-life scale demonstrated constructive methods, while large-scale models looked at how new spatial elements can be used.

Ito's work is underpinned by two principles: fluid spaces that give a tangible sense of dynamic force, and spaces that recall organic forms like trees and caves. The Kakamigahara Funeral Hall is an experimental building. Forms that tend to restore balance have been discarded in favour of forms that convey energy flows. Ito transforms Modernism's "less is more" into more natural spaces. The project is located in Gifu, a mountainous region north of Tokyo. Called "the forest of meditation" (Meiso no Mori), it was developed with Mutsuro Sasaki, the engineer who applies non-linear maths to structural engineering. (*Flux Structure*, published by Toto in 2005 and recently by the Architectural Academy of London, is a good introduction to his approach.) Sasaki talks of optimizing forces through a method called sensitivity analysis which assesses the solution providing the least stress and deformation during function.

Close collaboration between architect and engineering generates structural and spatial innovation. Creative ideas can be turned into reality using complex geometries and advanced software. Alongside his sensitivity analysis, Sasaki introduces the concept of "extended evolutionary structural optimization". By applying the principles of evolution and "self-organization" of living organisms to an engineering problem, rational computer-generated structural forms can be generated.

The method was first experimented with Arata Isozaki for the international competition for the large Beijing national theatre in 1998, and subsequently for the Kitagata Cultural Centre, realized, again with Isozaki, in 2005. Then came the Meiso no Mori Funeral Hall with Toyo Ito.

Mutsuro Sasaki has collaborated regularly with Ito, from his Sendai Mediatheque to today, even if Ito has also availed himself of people of the calibre of Cecil Balmond, Masato Araya and Masahiro Ikeda. Ito's structures are flowing entities. The Funeral Hall, for example, resembles a slowly forming cloud wafted by the breeze. The building is part of a large cemetery district inside a park and replaces a former construction. It overlooks a lake to the north and its large roof seems to extend from the hill rising behind it. The whole area was landscaped by Mikiko Ishikawa, professor at Keio University, and is conducive to quiet and reflection.

Inside, distribution is of the simplest. Beyond the large entrance, visitors access two areas where people pay their last respects to the dead, a corridor leading to three waiting rooms and a hall before the cremation precinct. The waiting rooms and large distribution corridor all look out onto the lake, bringing the landscape into the interior. All these spaces are contained under a broad roof supported by twelve thin conical columns. Some of them are placed on the exterior of the façade, creating another interesting mingling of indoors and outside. The glazed façade has wafer-thin frames, again minimizing the hiatus between interior and exterior and letting in the light. The second floor is occupied by plant and equipment above the cremation area.

The columns have built-in rainwater pipes and are one with the roof, which comprises four main sections of concave and convex shapes. The undulating design is based on an algorithm developed after lengthy computer processing. Floor slab thickness is a constant 8" (20 cm) throughout. The formwork for the walls is expertly wrought with sleepers, battens and support pillars. Each section of wall required a made-to-measure formwork design. The structure is at the same time roof and ceiling. The very few finishes are practically imperceptible to the eye, again helping to eliminate the distinction between inside and out. The upper section has a protective urethane resin coating, while the lower internal surfaces received a layer of thermal insulating mortar. The structure is white – like the cloud it resembles. And like a slowly moving cloud, volumes below the roof seem to dissolve in the air.

 XX Section - Scale 1:500

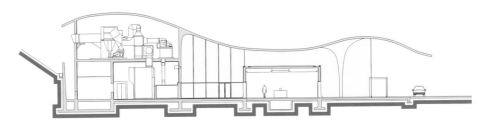

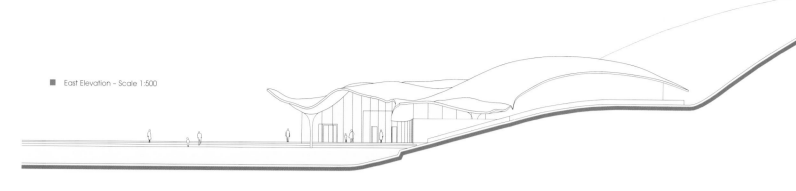

West Elevation – Scale 1:500

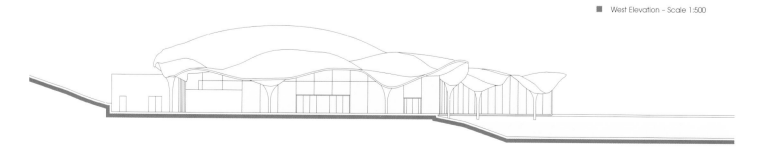

A

22

**DETAILS A AND B: FAÇADE,
ROOF AND COLUMN
VERTICAL SECTION – SCALE 1:15
HORIZONTAL SECTION – SCALE 1:10**

1. 1/8" (3 mm) resin-based mortar spray-painted with urethane-based water-repellent and anti-slip finish, 3/8" (10 mm) cement plaster, 7 7/8" (200 mm) reinforced concrete slab, heat-insulating mortar, 3/8" (10 mm) resin-based plaster
2. Reinforcing bar
3. L-shaped steel plate connecting façade to slab
4. Connecting steel plate
5. Connecting element
6. Galvanized steel profile
7. 3/16" (5 mm) steel plate finish
8. Silicone seal
9. FRP shell
10. Hot-painted 2 x 2" (50 x 50 mm) steel T-profile with male coupler, 1/2" (13 mm) silicone seal, 3/4" (19 mm) tempered glass, 1/2" (13 mm) silicone seal, hot-painted 2 x 2" (50 x 50 mm) steel T-profile with female coupler
11. 1/2" (12 mm) tapered steel plate
12. 3/8" (9 mm) steel plate joint
13. 5/8" (16 mm) thick steel clamps joining glass
14. 3/8 – 1/2" (9 – 12 mm) thick steel plates supporting façade system
15. Casing closing off bottom of façade formed by 3/16" (5 mm) aluminium plates

16. System of steel plates anchoring façade to slab
17. 1 5/8 x 1 5/8" (40 x 40 mm) steel L-profile
18. Channel for collecting condensation formed by 3/4 x 3/4" (20 x 20 mm) steel U-profiles
19. Reinforced concrete bracket beam
20. Reinforced concrete foundation with sprayed waterproofing
21. 3/4" (20 mm) thick 23 5/8 x 23 5/8" (600 x 600 mm) marble floor tiles, 1 1/8" (30 mm) levelling mortar, 3 1/8" (80 mm) screed, 3/4" (20 mm) board insulation, 7 7/8" (200 mm) reinforced concrete slab, 3 1/8" (80 mm) concrete base, 2 1/2" (60 mm) ballast layer, earth
22. Rainwater collection and filtering system
23. 3/8" (10 mm) resin-based plaster, reinforced concrete, steel captive nut anchoring reinforcement, 1/2" (12 mm) thick 8 1/2 x 8 1/2" (215 x 215 mm) box-shaped steel beam, Ø 4 1/2" (115 mm) interior steel drain pipe
24. 3/4" (19 mm) thick steel plate, 1 1/8" (30 mm) concrete footing, reinforced concrete foundation with sprayed waterproofing
25. Reinforcing and connecting steel plate
26. Steel plate supporting drain pipe
27. PVC cover
28. Ø 2 3/4" (70 mm) steel drain pipe
29. Concrete trench for collecting rainwater, 3 1/8" (80 mm) concrete base, layer of ballast

23

26

27

28

24

25

29

The Cube Tower, an office highrise in a new-development district of the Mexican city of Guadalajara, stands out for its high-quality, multi-functional character. It is the key feature of the burgeoning Jorge Vergara Cabrera (JVC) Centre which will also house a mix of cultural and commercial activities including museums, conference hall, trade fair, shopping centre and an urban park designed by Carme Pinós. A landmark in an urban fabric of non-descript buildings, the tower asserts itself as an icon of international architecture.

The "Cube" is not the usual parallelepiped-shaped office highrise. The singular composition turns site constraints into key design features. The starting point was to opt for a mixed structural system. As well as ensuring a building with lighter overall dead weight, as required by local earthquake regulations, the design also provides efficient vertical distribution and a rational pillar-less floor plan for all office floor space. The initial sketch outlined the main features of the project: a structure supported on three vertical elements in reinforced concrete, surrounded by a circular sequence of spaces and volumes. The horizontal section shows three parabola-shaped structural elements that generate convex and concave forms, on the exterior and interior respectively. At the centre, the scooped-out shapes of the three structural pillars create an entrance atrium of alternating concave masses and openings.

A huge central well allows natural light and air flows across the glazed façades. The outward-facing convex sides of each structural pillar contain staircases, lifts and ancillary services. Static problems were solved by using reinforced concrete to anchor the cantilevered steel beams in the vertical structures. These variable section beams are also connected to oblique and vertical members to provide further strengthening, and to support the floor slabs which were cast in place and craned into position. This system of external supports and struts allows for column-less, wall-to-wall open interiors.

Viewed as a whole, the building appears made up of three pieces. The office blocks are staggered trapezoid shapes, their shorter sides facing the inner court. Set like spokes around a hub, they cantilever outwards, the larger volumes on the outside. Three floors of each cantilevering block have been eliminated at different levels, in a staggered fashion to create covered terraces: in one, the first three floors are missing, in the other two, the gap is half way up. As well as lightening structure and design, the voids also facilitate air flow and natural lighting in the central tower court. The external elevations have double skins: an inner glazed façade with anodized aluminium frames, and an elegant outer envelope of sun-shading slats in treated northern pinewood, secured by a modular steel frame. Gaps in the brise-soleil skin leave exposed expanses of the full-height inner glazed walls. Metal grid walkways in the air space allow access to the façades for cleaning and maintenance.

Climate conditions in Guadalajara do not require the use of artificial air conditioning systems. Natural ventilation is sufficient, especially when, as in this case, the building encourages air circulation through the central tower well.

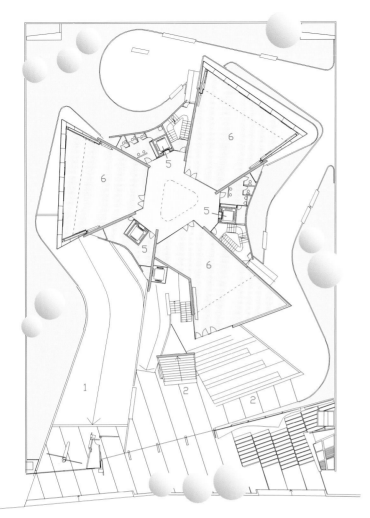

■ Ground Floor Plan – Scale 1:500

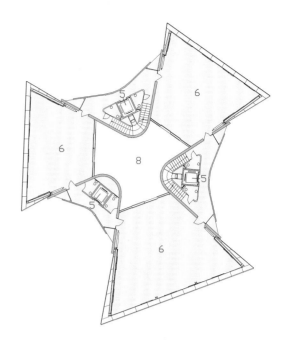

■ Typical Floor Plan – Scale 1:500

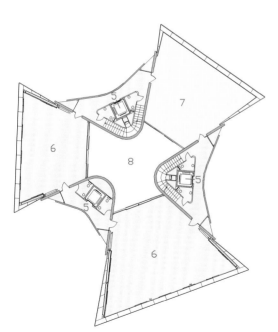

■ Fifth Floor Plan – Scale 1:500

1. Parking entrance
2. Entrance
3. Janitor's lodge
4. Central atrium
5. Staircase and lift
6. Offices
7. Terrace
8. Void

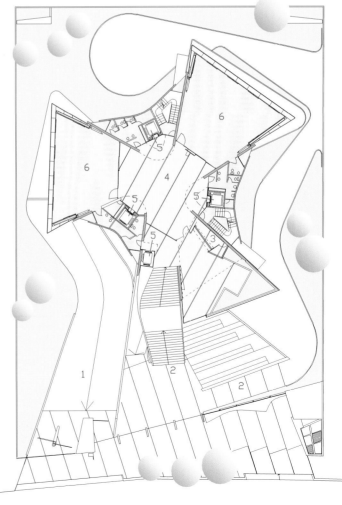

■ Atrium Plan – Scale 1:500

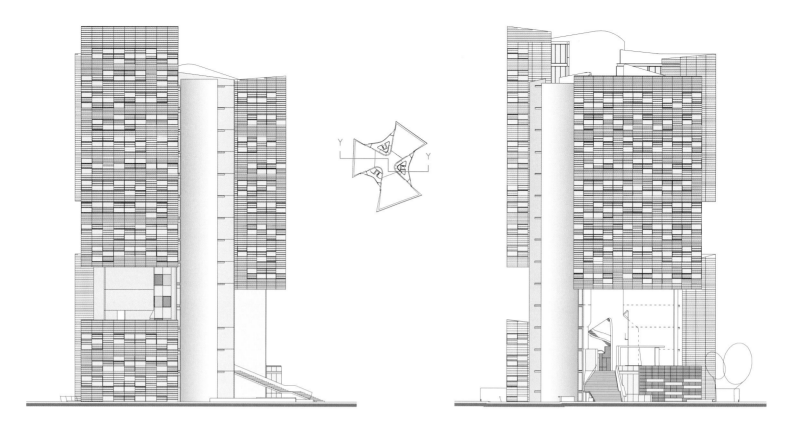

■ South Elevation – Scale 1:600

■ East Elevation – Scale 1:600

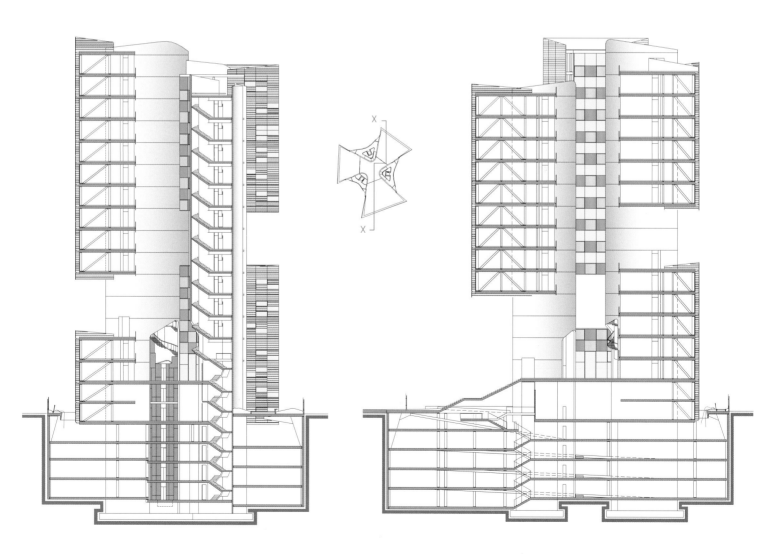

■ YY Section – Scale 1:600

■ XX Section – Scale 1:600

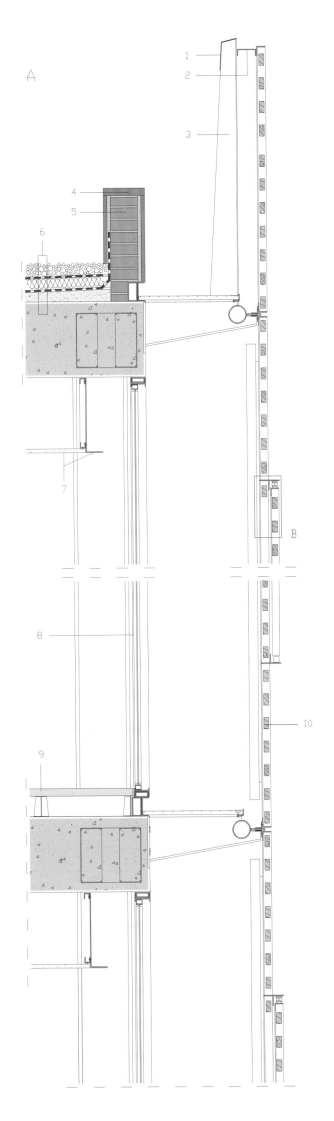

A

EXTERIOR FAÇADE
DETAIL A: VERTICAL SECTION
SCALE 1:20
DETAILS B, C AND D: VERTICAL SECTIONS
DETAILS E AND F: HORIZONTAL SECTIONS
SCALE 1:10

1. 3/16" (5 mm) thick steel flashing
2. 4 x 1 3/8" (101 x 36 mm) steel C-profile spacer
3. 6 1/8" (153 mm) max. H tapered stainless steel T-profile supporting brise-soleil panels
4. 1 5/8" (40 mm) thick Recinto volcanic rock cladding
5. Edging in 5 7/8" (150 mm) solid brick finished with 3/4" (20 mm) volcanic rock
6. Roof with 3/4" (20 mm) ballast, waterproofing membrane, 1 5/8" (40 mm) extruded polyurethane board insulation, waterproofing membrane, 2 3/8" (64 mm) max. H concrete screed forming slope, 15 3/4" (400 mm) compressed reinforced concrete slab
7. False ceiling in 3/4" (20 mm) gypsum board on frame of 1 1/8" x 1 1/8" (30 x 30 mm) galvanized steel C-profiles and 15 1/2 x 3 3/4" (395 x 95 mm) steel L-profile
8. Glazed façade formed by 1/4" (6 mm) glass and aluminium frame
9. Floating floor
10. Brise-soleil in wood slats on frame of 2 x 2" (50 x 50 mm) steel L-profiles and 4 3/8 x 2 1/8" (110 x 55 mm) steel t-profiles
11. 4 x 1/4" (102 x 6 mm) steel T-profile
12. Brise-soleil panel sliding mechanism
13. 5/16 x 1 1/2" (8 x 38 mm) steel supporting plate
14. 1 x 1 1/8" (25 x 30 mm) aluminium box-shaped profile fastening brise-soleil
15. 1 1/2 x 1 1/2" (38 x 38 mm) steel L-profile support (parallel to plane of section)
16. Brise-soleil in 1 1/8 x 2 1/2" (28 x 60 mm) heat-treated Nordic pine wood slats
17. Structure of steel box and C profiles supporting glazed façade
18. Façade maintenance walkway formed by galvanized steel grates
19. 1/2 x 3" (13 x 76 mm) steel plate connecting modular brise-soleil structure and pipe profile
20. Ø 4 1/8" (103 mm) steel pipe profile
21. 8 7/8" (227 mm) max. H steel bracket supporting modular structure of brise-soleil
22. 7 7/8 x 10 5/8 x 2 1/2" (200 x 270 x 60 mm) steel plate fastening bracket to slab
23. Ø 2 1/2" (60 mm) steel pipe profile
24. Ø 2" (50 mm) steel pipe profile
25. 2 x 2" (50 x 50 mm) aluminium profile support

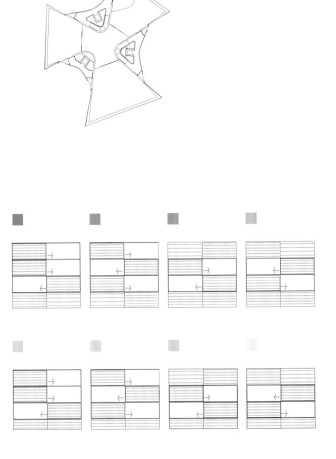

Façade modules
Elements with variable dimension

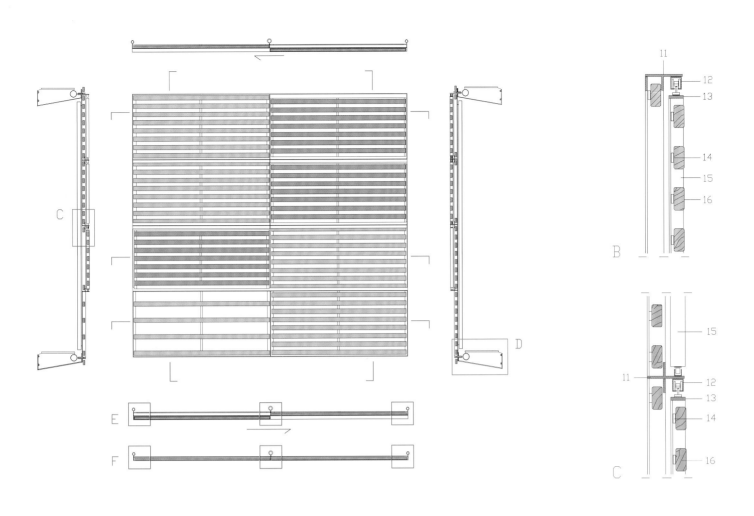

B

C

D

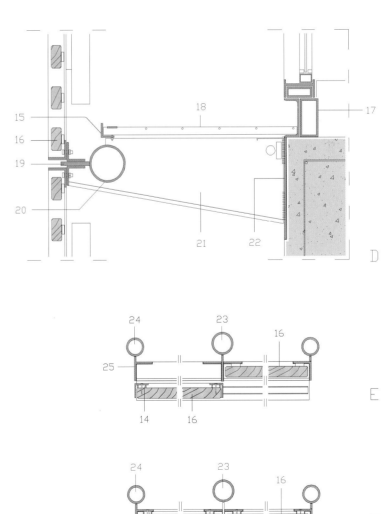

18

15

16

19

20

21   22

17

D

24   23   16

25

14   16

E

24   23   16

25

14   16

F

11

12

13

14

15

16

B

15

11

12

13

14

16

C

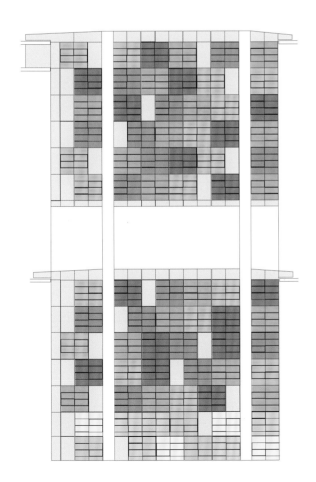

■ Brise-soleil façade modules scheme – Scale 1:500

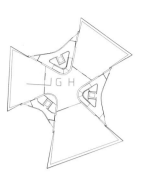

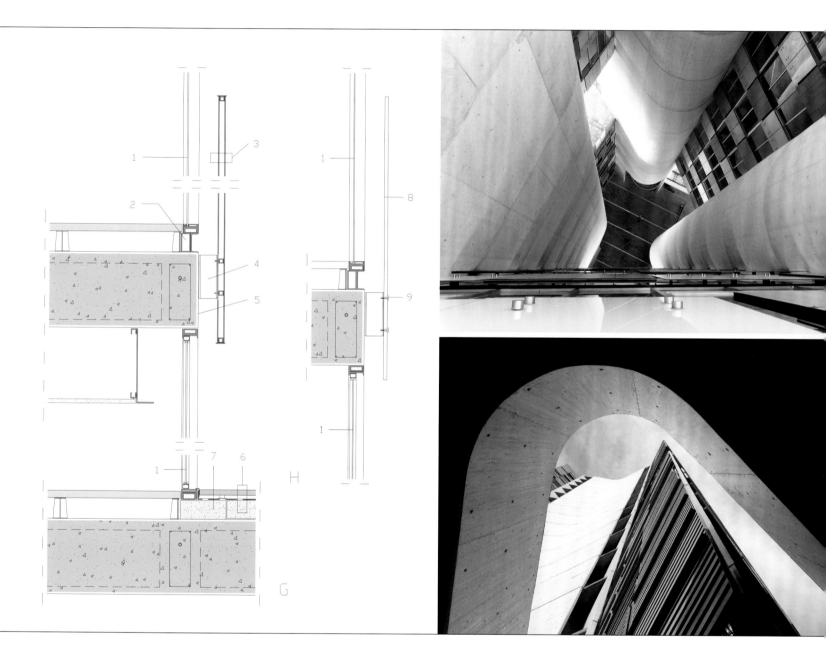

INTERIOR FAÇADE
DETAILS G AND H: VERTICAL SECTIONS
SCALE 1:20

1. Glazed façade with 1/8 + 1/8"
   (3 + 3 mm) transparent laminated
   glass and fixed and sliding
   aluminium frames
2. Structure of steel C- and
   box-shaped profiles supporting
   glazed façade and trim
3. Pair of light-coloured Prodema
   laminated wood panels with
   supporting frame of
   1 x 1" (25 x 25 mm) aluminium

   box-shaped profiles
4. 1 1/8 x 4 x 9 1/8" (30 x 100 x 230 mm)
   steel C-profile fastening
   wood panels to slab
5. Slab end with surface treatment
6. Flooring in 3/4" (20 mm)
   natural Recinto volcanic stone,
   waterproofing membrane,
   sloping lightweight concrete slab
7. Pre-cast concrete block supporting
   glazed façade on floor
8. 1/4 + 1/4" (6 + 6 mm) sheet
   of translucent glass
9. Stainless steel point
   fastener for glass

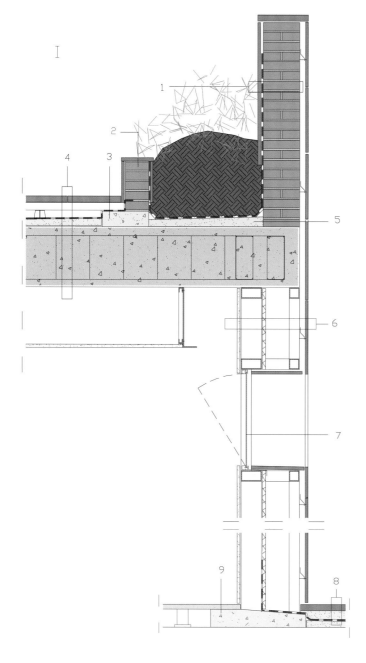

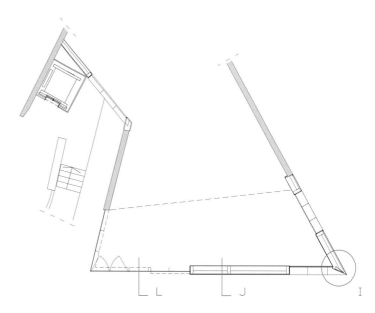

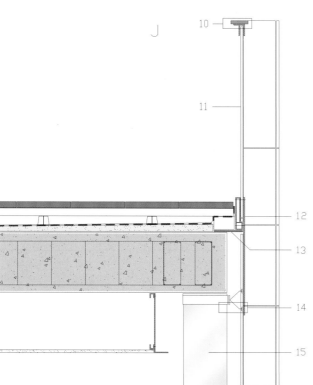

EXTERIOR ENTRANCE FAÇADE
DETAIL I: HORIZONTAL SECTION
DETAILS J AND L: VERTICAL SECTIONS
SCALE 1:25

1. 3/4" (20 mm) Recinto stone cladding, waterproofing membrane, dwarf wall in 9 7/8" (250 mm) solid brick
2. Edging in 5 7/8" (150 mm) solid brick
3. 12 5/8 x 4" (320 x 100 mm) pre-cast concrete block supporting edging
4. Floating floor in 1 5/8" (40 mm) Recinto stone tiles on 2" (50 mm) galvanized steel C-profiles (parallel to plane of section) and 2 1/4" (56 mm) galvanized steel L-profiles, waterproofing membrane, 1 3/4" (45 mm) concrete screed, 15 3/4" (400 mm) compressed reinforced concrete slab
5. 2 3/8" (64 mm) max. H lightweight concrete screed forming slope
6. 3/4" (20 mm) Recinto stone cladding on frame of 2 3/4 x 2 3/4" (70 x 70 mm) steel box-shaped profiles, 3/4" (20 mm) fireproof board insulation, frame of 5 12 x 2 3/4" (140 x 70 mm) steel box-shaped profiles, 3/4" (20 mm)

gypsum board finish
7. Transom window with 3/16" (5 mm) laminated glass and recessed aluminium frame
8. Flooring in 1 5/8" (40 mm) Recinto stone tiles, 2 3/8" (63 mm) dry concrete screed, waterproofing membrane, 1 5/8" (43 mm) max. H concrete screed forming slope
9. Pre-cast concrete block threshold
10. Upper finish of balustrade in 4 5/8 x 3/4" (120 x 20 mm) stainless steel plate and 3 1/8 x 3 1/8" (78 x 78 mm) stainless steel profile securing glass
11. 3/8" (10 mm) thick tempered glass balustrade
12. 10 1/4 x 3/8" (259 x 10 mm) steel plate with stainless steel box-shaped profiles supporting balustrade
13. 7 7/8 x 3/8" (200 x 10 mm) steel plate support
14. Glazed façade in 5/8" (15 mm) tempered glass with stainless steel supports
15. Vertical sheet of tempered glass supporting façade (parallel to plane of section)
16. Angle steel column with 3/4" (20 mm) thick Recinto volcanic stone cladding

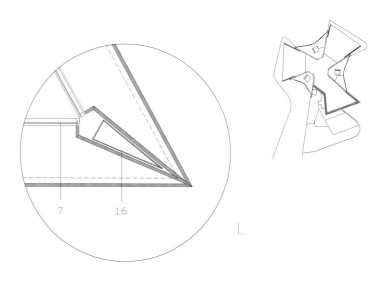

METZO COLLEGE
DOETINCHEM, THE NETHERLANDS

ERICK VAN EGERAAT
ASSOCIATED ARCHITECTS

The new Metzo College building in the city of Doetinchem in the east of the Netherlands houses a trade school and sports facility accessible to the public outside school hours. Completed in 2006 and winner of the Dutch award for new secondary school architecture, the complex replaces three previous schools and has a total surface area of 176,500 ft² (16,400 m²) catering for around 1,300 students aged between twelve and sixteen. Architect practice Erick van Egeraat developed a design in keeping with new thinking in vocational training. Accordingly, the architecture creates opportunities for interchange among student groups and accommodates the wide offering of practical and theoretical subjects, including health education and counselling.

A compact, square-shaped ground plan rises to form a six-storey truncated pyramid. A distinctive feature in an open, slightly undulating landscape dotted with trees, the building achieves a delicate balance between architectural landmark and harmonious addition to the countryside. The geometry of the elevations comprises prevalently horizontal lines crossed by oblique bands that make each façade distinctive. The alternation of cladding slabs and varying sized windows, together with a colour scheme that moves through tones of grey to ochre, help give a deliberate disjointedness to the elevations, breaking up the building's compact mass.

In deference to new educational concepts, the interior follows principles of flexibility, multi-functionality, transparency and openness. The ground plan provides open areas for group study and socialization, individual study corners and teacher workstations. Spaces and multi-functional classrooms can be redefined and reformulated to meet teaching requirements. The absence of stark divisions makes distribution within the various departments clearly legible.

The key feature is a central court-cum-patio. Placed above the entrance level, the court has a suspended ceiling whose external perimeter is an accessible roof garden, while the dropped-down central portion creates a patio flooded with natural daylight. Surrounded by study areas - the classrooms are located along the external perimeter - this large central space plays a key distribution and social role.

The school's public function is further enhanced by the accessibility of the sports facilities and restaurant to the general public. Conceived as an artificially lit "black box" on the underground levels, the gym has a separate entrance.

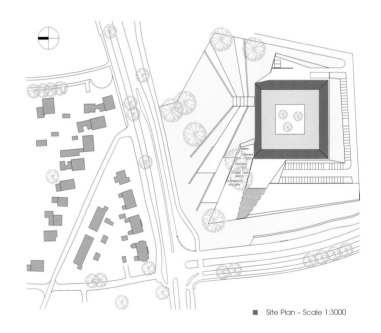

■ Site Plan – Scale 1:3000

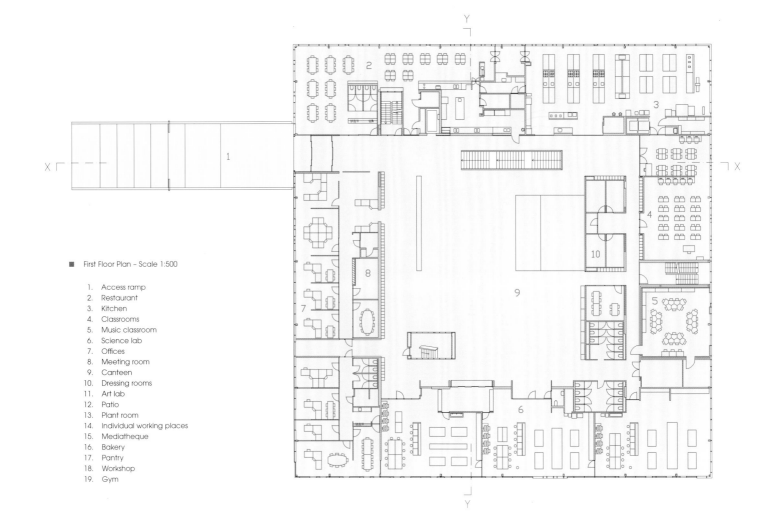

■ First Floor Plan – Scale 1:500

1. Access ramp
2. Restaurant
3. Kitchen
4. Classrooms
5. Music classroom
6. Science lab
7. Offices
8. Meeting room
9. Canteen
10. Dressing rooms
11. Art lab
12. Patio
13. Plant room
14. Individual working places
15. Mediatheque
16. Bakery
17. Pantry
18. Workshop
19. Gym

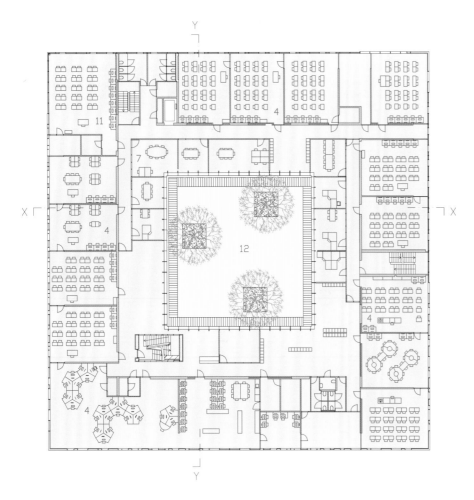

■ Third Floor Plan – Scale 1:500

■ West Elevation – Scale 1:500

18 · 4 · 4 · 4 · 4 · 6 · 4 · 3 · 4 · 18 · 18 · 18

■ South Elevation – Scale 1:500

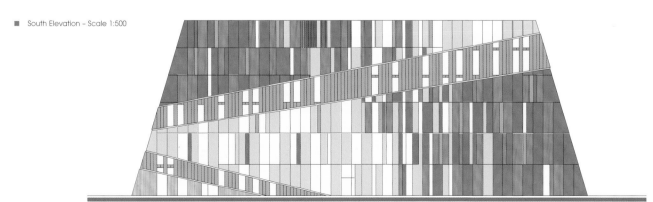

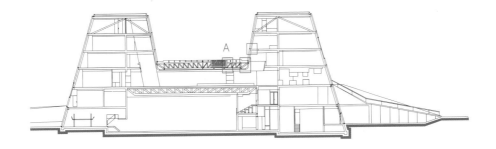

A

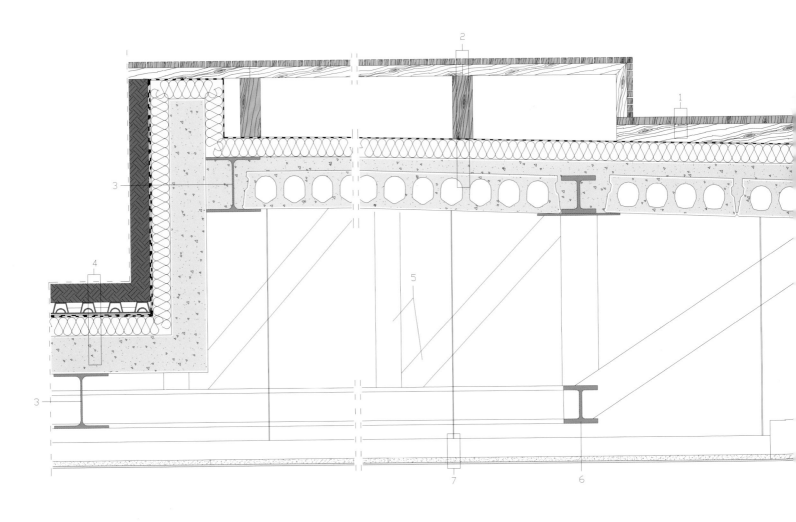

DETAIL A: CENTRAL PATIO
VERTICAL SECTION – SCALE 1:20

1. Perimeter walkway in 1 5/8"
   (40 mm) timber decking,
   shaped timber joist (parallel
   to plane of section)
2. Floating flooring in 1 1/8" (30 mm)
   timber boards, 2 1/2" (60 mm)
   timber joists (parallel to plane of
   section), timber beams of different
   heights, bituminous waterproofing
   membrane, 4" (100 mm)
   compression-resistant board
   insulation, 2 3/4" (70 mm)
   reinforced concrete slab, 7 7/8"
   (200 mm) prefabricated perforated
   reinforced concrete slab
3. HEA 300 steel beam with
   black fireproof paint

4. "ZinCo" substrate mix, 2 1/2"
   (60 mm) Floradrain drainage
   and aeration layer, protection
   mat, PVC waterproofing root
   barrier, bituminous waterproofing
   membrane, 4" (100 mm) board
   insulation, 7 7/8" (200 mm)
   prefabricated reinforced
   concrete pool
5. Trussed structure consisting of HEB
   140 steel profiles with fireproof paint
6. HEM 180 steel beam with
   fireproof paint
7. 3/8" (10 mm) plaster finish,
   1" (25 mm) gypsum board,
   4" (100 mm) steel C-profiles
   (parallel to plane of section)
   supporting gypsum board on
   tie rods connected to slab
8. 7 1/8" (180 mm) shaped steel

C-profile (parallel to plane of
section) supporting gypsum board
9. HEA 260 steel beam
   with fireproof paint
10. 5/8" (16 mm) thick steel
    plate cover on slab
11. Connecting element between
    patio and façade consisting
    of 1/2" (12 mm) plywood panel,
    4" (100 mm) insulation fill,
    3/4" (18 mm) plywood panel,
    waterproofing membrane
12. Continuous glazed façade
    with 5/16 – 1/2 – 1/4 + 1/4"
    (8 – 14 – 6.5 + 6.5 mm)
    double-glazing units
    with aluminium frames
13. 1/8" (4 mm) thick folded sheet
    steel external finish on slab
14. 3 1/8" x 1 5/8 (80 x 40 mm)

aluminium box-shaped
profile supporting finish
15. 4" (100 mm) thick
    acoustic insulation panel
16. 5 7/8" x 2" (150 x 50 mm) aluminium
    box-shaped profile internally
    insulated with fibreglass
17. Epoxy resin flooring, 2 3/4"
    (70 mm) screed, 2 3/4" (70 mm)
    reinforced concrete slab, 10
    1/4" (260 mm) prefabricated
    perforated reinforced concrete
    slab, 2 3/4" (70 mm) fibreglass
    board insulation on frame of
    2 3/4" x 2" (70 x 50 mm) wood
    with fireproofing treatment, folded
    sheet aluminium finish on slab
18. Sealant tape
19. 3/16" (5 mm) thick folded
    sheet steel finish on slab

DETAIL B: FAÇADE SYSTEM
VERTICAL SECTION – SCALE 1:20

1. Double waterproofing membrane, 2 3/4" (70 mm) Vaportherm XR board insulation, 4" (100 mm) screed, 2 3/4" (70 mm) reinforced concrete slab, 12 5/8" (320 mm) prefabricated perforated reinforced concrete slab
2. Double waterproofing membrane, 3/4" (18 mm) plywood panel, insulation fill, 3/4" (18 mm) plywood panel, waterproofing membrane, white anodized aluminium flashing
3. Aluminium profile finish supporting flashing
4. White anodized aluminium flashing
5. Steel system anchoring façade to slab
6. 2 1/8" (55 mm) rockwool board insulation covered by shaped sheet steel
7. Roller blind providing sun protection for façade
8. Operable window with aluminium frame and 5/16 – 1/2 – 1/4 + 1/4" (8 – 14 – 6.5 + 6.5 mm) double glazing
9. 3/16" (5 mm) steel L-profile finish on bottom of slab
10. Sealant tape
11. Façade in 5 7/8 x 2" (150 x 50 mm) box-shaped aluminium profiles internally insulated with fibreglass
12. Stud (parallel to plane of section), 5/16" (8 mm) security glass, 2 1/8" (55 mm) ventilated airspace, 1/16" (2 mm) painted sheet aluminium, vapour barrier, 2 3/4" (70 mm) Vaportherm XR board insulation, frame of 2 x 1 5/8" (50 x 40 mm) steel C-profiles supporting gypsum board (parallel to plane of section), double 1" (25 mm) gypsum board, 11 3/4 x 7 7/8" (300 x 200 mm) steel column (parallel to plane of section)
13. Aluminium skirting
14. 1" (25 mm) bronze-copper coloured fibrecement cladding, 1" (25 mm) foamed polyurethane board insulation, vapour barrier, 2 3/4" (70 mm) Vaportherm XR board insulation
15. Polyurethane panel covered with sheet aluminium
16. Epoxy resin flooring, 2 3/4" (70 mm) concrete screed, 1 5/8" (40 mm) Vaportherm XR board insulation, 11 3/4" (300 mm) reinforced concrete slab
17. 19 3/4" (500 mm) reinforced concrete structure, 4" (100 mm) polyurethane board insulation, waterproofing membrane, earth

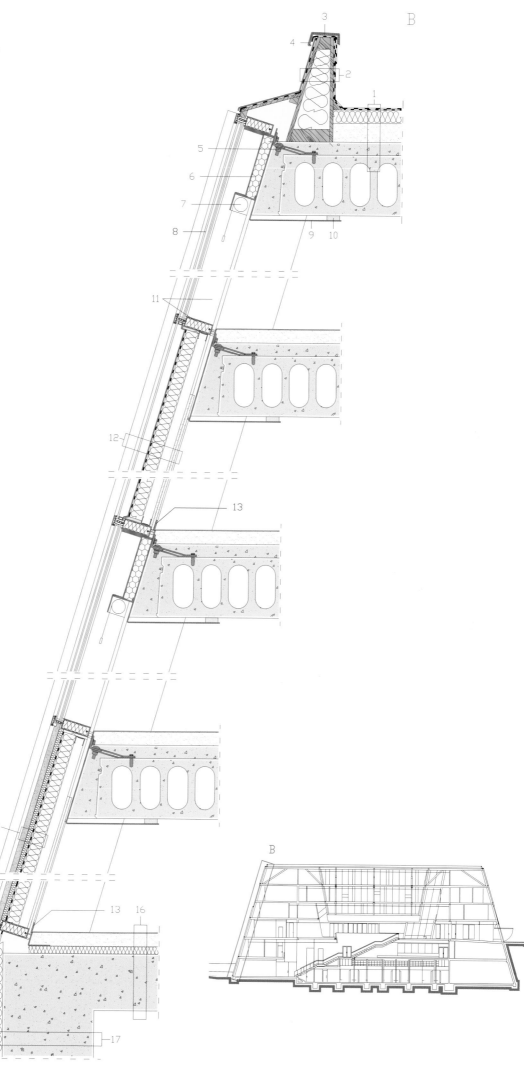

SHIPPING AND TRANSPORT COLLEGE
ROTTERDAM, THE NETHERLANDS

NEUTELINGS & RIEDIJK

The whole process is predicated on an intuition. Appearance, form and primary exterior features, even the building's function and liveability all take their cue from an initial leap of the imagination. Yet though Neutelings & Riedijk let their instinct define the character of the building – light-hearted, ironic, yet monumental – its realization is the result of meticulously detailed creative programming. They break down client requirements, examine the possibilities and determinate which aspects deserve more time and money. It is a synthesis of pragmatism and ecstasy where the architect, he who gives form to client demands, becomes the creator of value added.

It is no surprise that Neutelings & Riedijk define their buildings as "sculptures". The profile of the Shipping and Transport College is a lighthouse, an intangible beacon along the river, a watchtower over the sea and an observation tower over the future city. Part of the regeneration project for the port of Rotterdam, the College stands out on the city's skyline, an unmistakable landmark to optimism. Even the choice of putting a maritime school in a tower, to obtain precious space, flies in the face of convention. The structure is easy to read: a single element bends in on itself at the top to create a cantilevered auditorium, and then bends twice at ground level to end in a spectacular picture window overlooking the river. Prefabricated concrete slabs form the main structure. These are clad in a chequerboard of undulated aluminium panels that lend an air of impermanence to the whole building, as if it were a stack of containers soon to be shipped out.

Once past the threshold, what Neutelings & Riedijk call "Scenario" becomes immediately evident. Spatial organization blends a series of completely diverse functions and creates opportunities for people of different backgrounds but common interests to come together. Internal spaces are articulated to give as much emphasis as possible to public spaces, in the most social sense of the word. Scenario is also evident in the particular character given to each environment.

Even the furniture has been designed by the architects in a clear effort to create an all-enveloping atmosphere and plan every aspect of their work. The student canteen, with its huge picture window overlooking river and shipping, resembles the galley of a ship. Private offices could be first-class cabins, hallways and access areas early twentieth century customs areas. This is no mere play on metaphors, however, but a means of creating clear distinctions between the many settings contained in a single building. The presence of so many different functions in the same place (mechanical workshops, virtual simulation labs, gym, restaurants, auditorium, cafeteria, offices, bookstore, wc, library) and the constant view of the sea gives you the impression you are on a transatlantic liner about to sail.

Knowing that the budget would allow no luxuries, Neutelings & Riedijk concentrated on spatial development, creating outstanding environments like the restaurants and auditorium to take the tedium out of the agonizingly slow escalators. Their building is further confirmation that their planning model can fully meet client demands and prompt creativity even within a complex project like this. It especially brings out to the full their playful irreverent humour, and their ability as architects to create references with meaning for cities where the public and private sphere seem increasingly to clash.

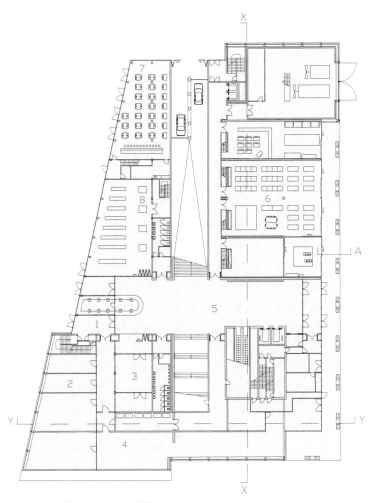

■ Ground Floor Plan – Scale 1:700

■ First Floor Plan – Scale 1:700

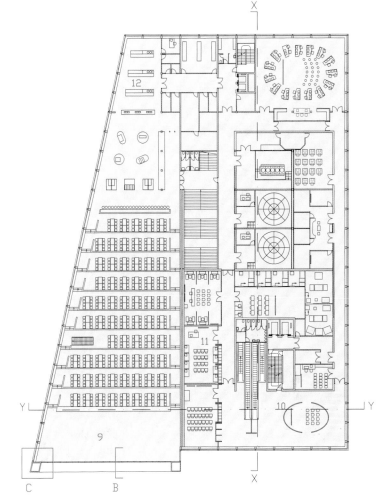

■ First Floor Plan – Scale 1:700

■ Second Floor Plan – Scale 1:700

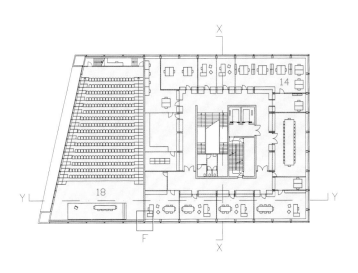

1.	Entrance	10.	Classrooms
2.	Printshop	11.	Simulation rooms
3.	Exhibition space	12.	Kitchen
4.	Cycle storage	13.	Media centre
5.	Hall	14.	Offices
6.	Workshops	15.	Sportshall
7.	Cafe	16.	Dressing rooms
8.	Bookshop	17.	Staff restaurant
9.	Student restaurant	18.	Auditorium

■ Fourteenth Floor Plan – Scale 1:700

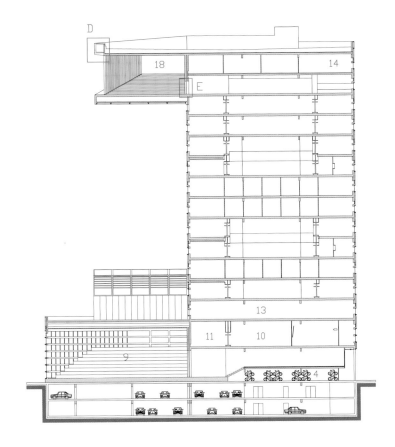

■ YY Section – Scale 1:700

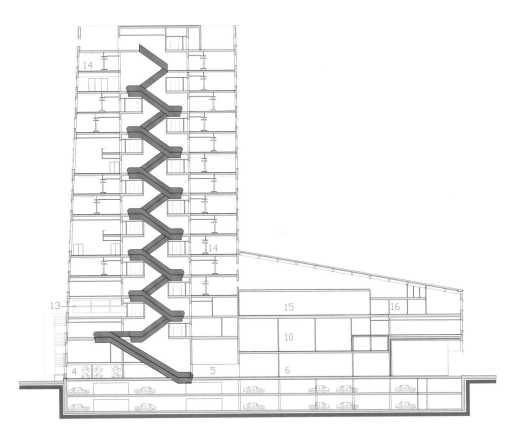

■ XX Section – Scale 1:700

INTERVIEW WITH WILLEM JAN NEUTELINGS

Emiliano Gandolfi - Part of the gradual revitalization of the port of Rotterdam, the Shipping and Transport College is the ultimate "urban icon", not at all what one would expect of a school building. How did it come about?

Willem Jan Neutelings - We had to bear in mind the particular character of the College, created fifteen years before from the merger of several Dutch maritime training establishments. The new school brought many completely different functions under the same roof: mechanical workshops, virtual simulation labs, restaurants, gyms, offices and classrooms. The result was a highly intricate programme. The College is also of international standing, so it was essential to develop a strong, recognizable image. Another key aspect was the need to maintain a visual reference with the port, its warehouses, silos and containers. This led us to propose a tower shape in keeping with a port environment. The form brings together all the requirements of the brief and at the same time gave us a highly distinctive building whose cantilevered auditorium offers splendid views over the sea.

E.G. - Is it true to say that you adopted the traditional school layout – central corridor with classrooms on each side – only you set it vertically? Is your architecture often so uninhibited?

W.J.N. - We firmly believe in the store of knowledge architecture provides and in using the typical instruments of our profession. It's like a doctor who will use the best treatment for his patient. We have thousands of years' worth of spatial organization solutions we can use in the contemporary context. The Rotterdam College, for example, took one particular typology and turned it into something completely different. Had we adopted the traditional approach we would never have won the competition, simply because it was not the right answer to the problem. Using the tools of architecture and transforming them for the specific situation is a fundamental element of our work.

E.G. - One of the most fascinating aspects of your work is how you are able to balance a pragmatic constructive approach with a touch of irony. How do you manage to include these extremes in your creative process?

W.J.N. - We asked ourselves the same question last year, and decided to organize the answer in *At Work*, a book on how we approach a project. In doing this study we realized that, to understand our creative process, we would have to collect and re-examine the drawings and models of the previous ten years. As a result we discovered we make constant use of sixteen actions, or themes – which then became the chapters of our book: things like Sculpture, Context, System and others. The procedure is simple. We always try to concentrate on formulating an effective concept that will accompany us throughout the whole planning process. We will apply one theme rather than another depending on the project, but we never start from a pre-constituted format or by choosing a material. The chapters of *At Work* are deliberately not numbered so as not to give any hierarchical order to the themes. Sometimes we use the right side of our brains, at other times, the left side, but in the end we always try to blend the two attitudes and let them mutually influence the various phases of the project.

E.G. - So once you have determined an effective concept, how do you proceed?

W.J.N. - The next step is to blend this system with architecture, an essentially sculpturing process making polyurethane models. Once we have defined the form, all we have to do then is look at the specific features of the particular environment. It's essential to compose a sequence of atmosphere like a sequence of settings. We try to study all the sequences of movements taking place within the building and trigger different emotions. We tend to create evocative stimuli: the escalators have the atmosphere of a submarine, the students' canteen feels like you're in a ship's galley, the teaching staff restaurant is like a luxury cabin.

E.G. - So to sum up, you start from the form in relation to a context and the client's requirements. Then you concentrate on the organization, and after that on a sensory programme. That leaves the external finishing.

W.J.N. - Yes, in the initial phase, the study of the form is always done on unfinished models. We consider the outer dressing only subsequently. This is the moment when we carry out careful research into materials and details. We do many studies to understand how to apply a certain pattern in the best possible way. We experiment with tactile qualities, trying to understand how form is perceived differently depending on the depth and size of the weave or grain. With the College, we wanted to mute the sense of the building's scale, so we avoided giving a perception of the various floors, using a large chequerboard scheme to highlight the profile. The partly perforated corrugated aluminium panels we chose recall the visual images of a port and its containers. In other words, the skin is functional to form, fitting with this particular building type.

E.G. - Your buildings usually have a striking materiality, which runs counter to current trends towards lightness and dematerialization. I believe that parallel to this you are doing special research into the use of light.

W.J.N. - Basically, we don't like "light" buildings. Constructions are heavy things that obey the laws of gravity. I don't understand why they must look like aeroplanes or ships! The use of light is another all-important aspect. I don't find transparent buildings very interesting: too much light and a unrelieved view onto the outside. Architecture is born of the contrast between light and shadow. Just think of the Pantheon in Rome. A little opening creates an extraordinary play of light. We conceive our buildings as completely dark units. Only subsequently do we start making small apertures. We prefer to soften light and sharpen sensory perception by alternating light and shadow.

E.G. - Living in your buildings always brings surprises. There are the differences in temperature, and the unusual use of common materials.

W.J.N. - Architecture should not just be developed for the eyes alone, or planned only for visual perception. It's not just a question of spaces but also sensations. It's essential to consider the tactile aspect, temperature, smells, sounds. We also try to get a different perception of outside noises, again with the idea of creating a wide spectrum of different perceptions. Another element given much attention is the climatic conditions in our buildings. The College has loggias on every second floor. They serve as places to congregate, and a place where you can perceive the outside atmosphere.

E.G. - The College had a fairly low budget, around 1200 Euro/sqm. How did you ensure high building standards and keep costs down?

W.J.N. - Usually we are obliged to have medium-quality finishing and we can hardly ever afford costly materials like stone. Moreover in Holland, construction is heavily industrialized and we are usually forced to used pre-assembled elements. So we try to use prefabricated units creatively, often turning the way conventional materials are used on its head.

E.G. - Is this unconventional use of materials part of your ironic take on architecture?

W.J.N. - No, that is a basic misconception. We are always asked at every conference whether our buildings are provocations, and we always reply no. We take our profession very seriously. We consider society and the effects that our buildings have very seriously indeed. At the same time, however, we don't take ourselves very seriously! Unfortunately many architects do the opposite. They take themselves terribly seriously but not the client or society. They are usually more interested in their artistic persona. Our drawings have nothing that is intentionally flippant. They reflect our thoughts on the role of architecture. We think that architecture should make people happier, and their lives more pleasant, perhaps even simpler. We don't want to fall into the area of difficult, at times even dramatic visions.

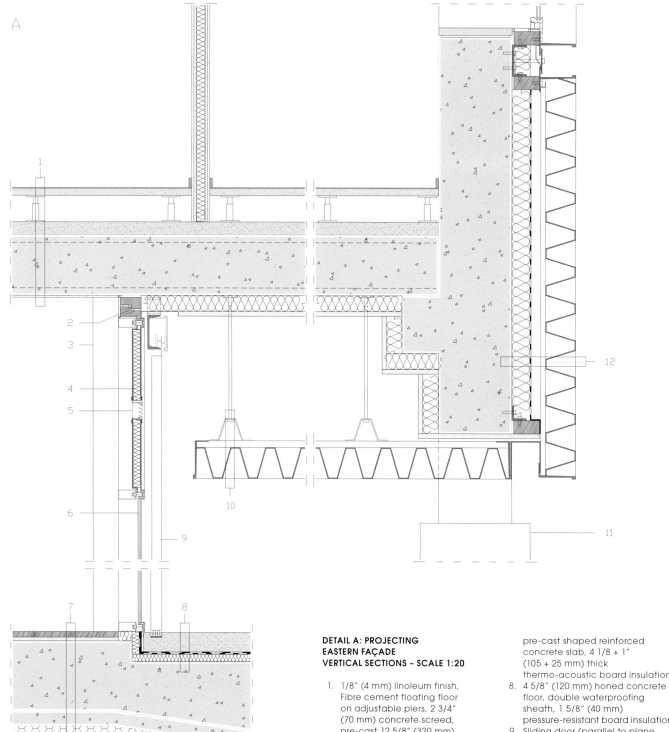

A

**DETAIL A: PROJECTING
EASTERN FAÇADE
VERTICAL SECTIONS – SCALE 1:20**

1. 1/8" (4 mm) linoleum finish,
    Fibre cement floating floor
    on adjustable piers, 2 3/4"
    (70 mm) concrete screed,
    pre-cast 12 5/8" (320 mm)
    reinforced concrete slab,
    3/8" (10 mm) plaster
2. Timber beam framework
3. Painted steel column (parallel
    to plane of section)
4. 2" (50 mm) thick sheet
    aluminium and
    insulation sandwich panel infill
5. Aluminium ventilation grille
6. Continuous glazed façade
    with 2 x 4" (50 x 100 mm)
    steel box frame and
    1/4 – 5/16 – 1/4" (6 – 8 – 6 mm)
    double glazing
7. 1 1/8" (30 mm) oak flooring,
    3/4" (20 mm) subfloor,
    14 1/2" (370 mm) reinforced
    concrete slab, 3 1/2" (80 mm)

pre-cast shaped reinforced
concrete slab, 4 1/8 + 1"
(105 + 25 mm) thick
thermo-acoustic board insulation

8. 4 5/8" (120 mm) honed concrete
    floor, double waterproofing
    sheath, 1 5/8" (40 mm)
    pressure-resistant board insulation
9. Sliding door (parallel to plane
    of section) with steel tracks
10. Corrugated sheet aluminium
    panel with blue and silver
    mica finish on 6 1/2" (165 mm)
    aluminium frame, 1 3/8" (35 mm)
    aluminium frame hung from slab
    by aluminium tie rods
11. V-shaped reinforced concrete
    column with 23 5/8 x 29 1/2"
    (600 x 750 mm) section
12. Corrugated sheet aluminium
    panel with blue and silver mica
    finish on 6 1/2" (165 mm) aluminium
    frame, 1 1/4" (32 mm)
    supporting metal upright,
    waterproofing membrane,
    4" (100 mm) insulation layer,
    reinforced concrete edge beam

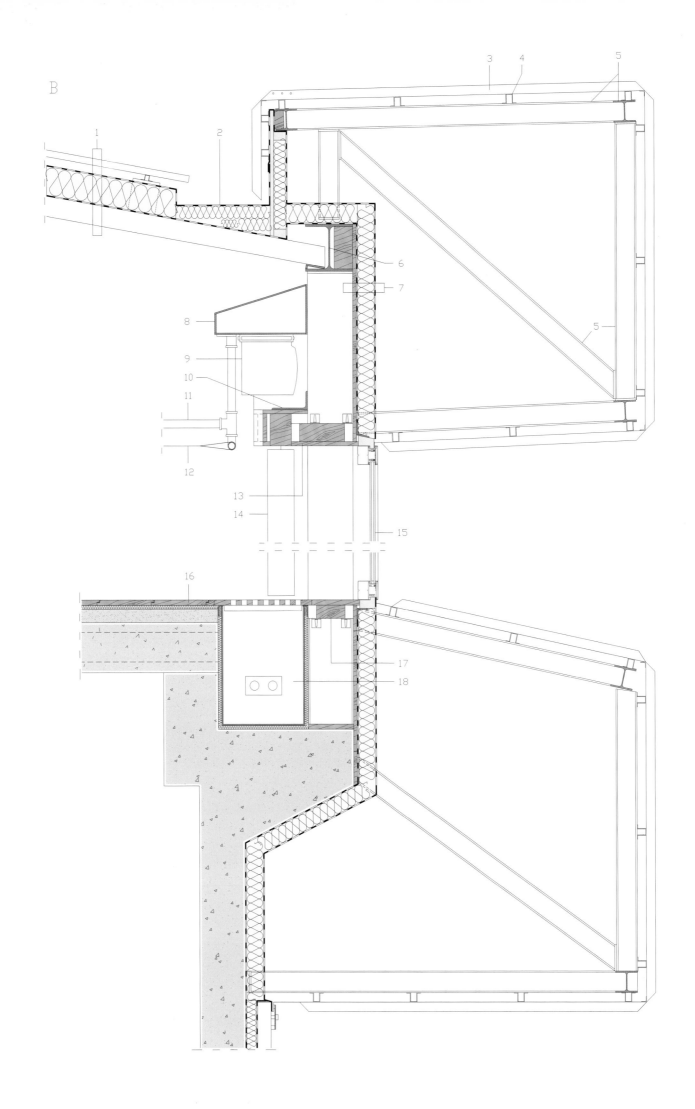

B

1
2
3
4
5
5
6
7
8
9
10
11
12
13
14
15
16
17
18

C

3

19

15

5

4

**DETAILS B, C AND D (OVERLEAF):
FAÇADE CONSTRUCTION SYSTEM
VERTICAL AND HORIZONTAL SECTIONS
SCALE 1:20**

1. Corrugated sheet aluminium
   roofing on 1 1/8" (30 mm) H steel
   omega profiles, waterproofing
   membrane, 5 7/8" (150 cm)
   board insulation, vapour barrier,
   false ceiling in corrugated sheet
   aluminium panel with blue
   and silver mica finish on 6 1/2"
   (165 mm) aluminium frame
2. Rainwater gutter
3. Compression-joined sheet
   aluminium cladding
4. Ø 2" (50 mm) metal profile
5. Frame of HEA 120 steel beams
6. HEA 240 steel beam
7. Waterproofing membrane,
   4" (100 mm) board insulation,
   vapour barrier,
   7/8" (22 mm) MDF panel,
   9 7/8 x 5 7/8" (250 x 150 mm)
   steel box column (parallel
   to plane of section)
8. Shaped steel box beams
9. Protective roller screen
10. 7 7/8 x 4" (200 x 100 mm)
    steel L-profile
11. Structure of Ø 1 5/8" (40 mm)
    steel pipes supporting
    suspended ceiling

12. Suspended ceiling in raw
    hemp in natural colour suspended
    under tension by supporting
    pipes with metal cable
13. 7/8" (22 mm) MDF fascia board
14. Vertical sun blinds
15. Continuous glazed façade
    with 5/16 – 1/2 – 5/16"
    (8 – 12 – 8 mm) aluminium
    double-glazing units
16. 1 1/8" (30 mm) thick
    wood tile flooring
17. Sub-structure in 2 3/4 x 6 1/4"
    (70 x 160 mm) wood beams
18. Heat converter installation space
19. 4" (100 mm) H metal Z-profile
20. Façade maintenance installation
21. HEM 1000 steel beam
22. Waterproofing membrane,
    7/8" (22 mm) MDF panel,
    4" (100 mm) board insulation
    7/8" (22 mm) MDF panel
23. Roof waterproofing membrane,
    12 5/8" (320 mm) board insulation,
    rockwool of variable thicknesses,
    4 1/8" (106 mm)
    H corrugated sheeting
    with fibreglass fill
24. 47 1/4 x 47 1/4" (1200 x 1200 mm)
    padded panels finished
    in red imitation leather,
    suspended ceiling frame
    in wood suspended from
    beams by steel tie rods

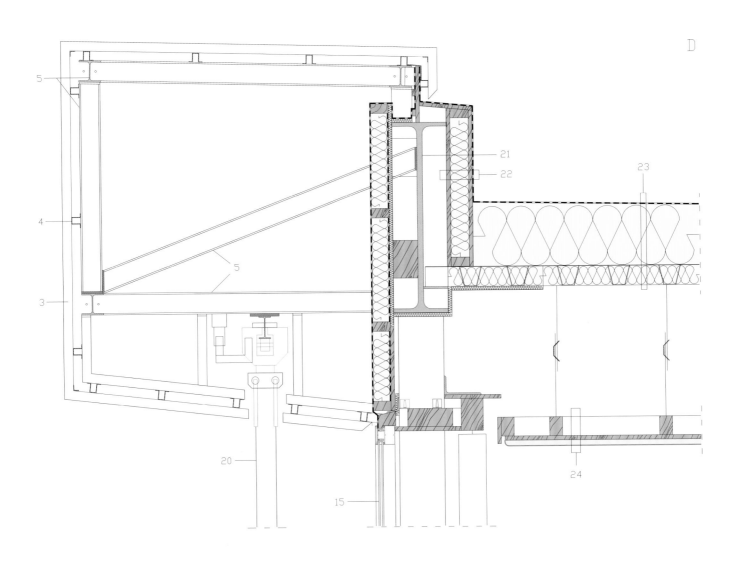

D

5

4

3

5

21

22

23

20

15

24

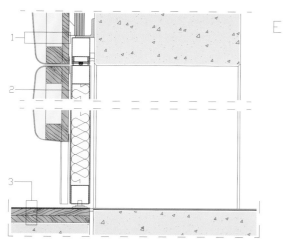

E

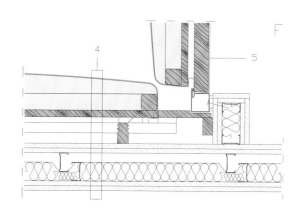

F

DETAILS E AND F: CONFERENCE ROOM INTERIOR FINISH VERTICAL AND HORIZONTAL SECTIONS SCALE 1:10

1. 47 1/4 x 47 1/4" (1200 x 1200 mm) padded panels finished in imitation leather on wood frame
2. Laminated aluminium door with 2" (50 mm) thick mineral wool acoustic insulation
3. 1 1/8" (30 mm) black rubber

matting, double 1 3/8" (36 mm) plywood panels
4. 47 1/4 x 47 1/4" (1200 x 1200 mm) padded panels finished in red imitation leather on wood frame, double 1" (25 mm) gypsum board, 1" (25 mm) air space with metal uprights, 2" (50 mm) board insulation, double 1" (25 mm) gypsum board
5. Wood door

26.09.98

Galway-Mayo Institute of Technology, GMIT, is located on the approach road to Galway City, along the Dublin Road. The site is due south and overlooks Galway Bay. The former campus reflected standard seventies regional-college architecture with pre-cast concrete cladding panels, ribbon windows and no sense of identity. GMIT wanted to create a new landmark frontage, a building that responded to environmental conditions while referring to and utilizing local materials. The palette of materials used includes painted render, native limestone and patinated copper. Copper was chosen for its vibrant colour and malleable qualities, best suited to the organic forms that contrast with the orthogonal building elements.

The building comprises two rectangular volumes: the Lecture Block and the Library-IT Block. The Lecture Block consists of sixteen lecture theatres and auditoria of varying capacities stacked above each other over three levels, with the Administration Department set back at roof level on one side. In the adjacent block, the IT Department is topped by the two stacked levels of the library which are connected by a gluelam beech central staircase.

The main entrance occurs where these two volumes overlap, demarcating the new axial route through the existing college. The centre fits within a contoured landscape with ground levels rising and falling around its perimeter, mirroring the footprint of the building. A triangular wedge of land addresses the difference in level between the new and existing buildings, rising towards the GMIT with a cantilevered bridge connecting to the main entrance. A purple, free-form fabric canopy stretches across the bridge, sheltering it from southwesterly winds.

A cast-in-situ mass concrete wall links the two rectangular forms, denoting the primary line of movement through the building. At the library end of this wall, a series of three-pin steel portal frames push out

a layer of the Library-IT enclosure which recedes into the landscape, creating a more organic edge. This edge segments into three copper-clad forms, shielding the library areas from solar gain and acting as acoustic baffles and light reflectors.

Framed views of Galway Bay are strategically gained at the sail junctions where stainless steel strip windows are inserted. The free-form compositions reflect the shape of trapezoidal sails and take cognizance of Galway's location on the shores of the Atlantic Ocean and its maritime past. The three wide sculptured copper sails act as large air dispensers and form part of the library's natural ventilation strategy. Form intertwines function to dictate the final modelling of the sails' cross section.

The library interior reflects the organic external forms. Racked columns push 'islands' of floor plane towards the sails. At the east end of the library, the floor plane fractures to create trapezoidal voids through which light filters to the lower library floor where the majority of the book stacks are located. The concept is developed further at roof level with glazed elements peeling off the roof plane as if suspended in thin air. The library space is enclosed by a glazed wall that runs from the end copper sail right to the flat façade. Steel trusses emphasize the horizontal lines along this glazed surface, creating a structure that seems to be restraining the sails in the wind.

The natural daylight that filters into the building at 360 degrees continuously "remodels" the interior as the sun changes angle. The design uses architectural elements as orientation devices, the building form to zone its functions, its skin to control the environment and the use of materials as a hierarchical index. Sculptured, patinated copper forms enclose one of the most important spaces on the campus, the library, and occur strategically at the most public corner of the campus.

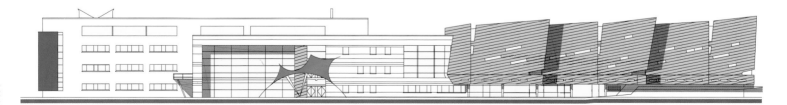

■ South Elevation – Scale 1:800

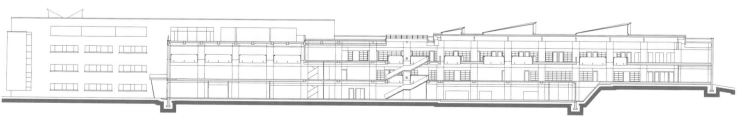

■ Longitudinal Section – Scale 1:800

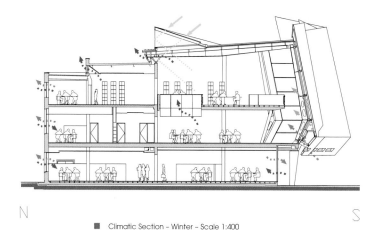

■ Climatic Section – Winter – Scale 1:400

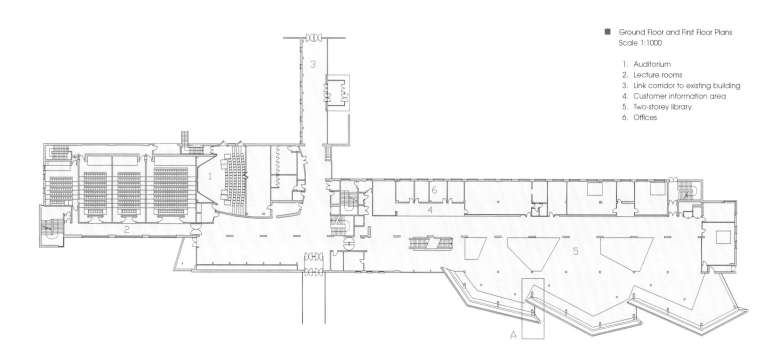

■ Ground Floor and First Floor Plans
Scale 1:1000

1. Auditorium
2. Lecture rooms
3. Link corridor to existing building
4. Customer information area
5. Two-storey library
6. Offices

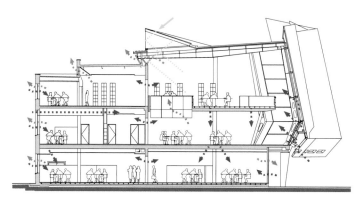

■ Climatic Section – Summer – Scale 1:400

Reference Section
X Y Z Details – Scale 1:200

DETAILS A (P. 177) AND B:
CONSTRUCTION SYSTEM OF SAILS
HORIZONTAL AND VERTICAL SECTIONS
SCALE 1:40

1. Ballast layer, waterproofing membrane, 4" (100 mm) rockwool board insulation, vapour barrier, 1 1/8" (30 mm) board insulation, 3 1/8" (80 mm) micro-perforated corrugated plannja panel, 9 7/8 x 4" (250 x 100 mm) steel box beam
2. Steel flashing
3. 11 3/4 x 4" (300 x 100 mm) steel box beam
4. Structural system comprising hinged tapered steel beams
5. Steel connecting hinge
6. Steel plate connecting façade structure to load-bearing structure, 3/4" (20 mm) MDF boarding, 1" (25 mm) plywood beams, vapour barrier, 2 1/2" (60 mm) rockwool board insulation, 7 7/8 x 7 7/8" (200 x 200 mm) secondary steel I-beam with reinforcing wood beams, wood upright (parallel to plane of section), 1" (25 mm) wood beams, waterproofing membrane, copper cladding pre-patinated Tecu patina cladding
7. Steel profile cover
8. Fixed window with steel frame and double glazing
9. Fixed ventilation grille
10. 3/4" (20 mm) MDF boarding, 1" (25 mm) plywood beams, vapour barrier, board insulation, wood upright (parallel to plane of section)
11. Adjustable ventilation grille
12. Ventilation and heating system
13. Pre-patinated Tecu patina cladding, 1" (25 mm) wood beams, plywood panel, vapour barrier, steel C-profile with reinforcing wood beam
14. Reinforced concrete beam
15. Flooring in 3/8" (10 mm) acoustic insulating cork, 1 5/8" (40 mm) screed, 7 7/8" (200 mm) pre-cast reinforced concrete slab, vapour barrier, 3 1/8" (80 mm) board insulation
16. Aluminium cladding on frame of steel Z-profiles
17. Reinforced concrete column
18. Ventilation grille with copper fly screen

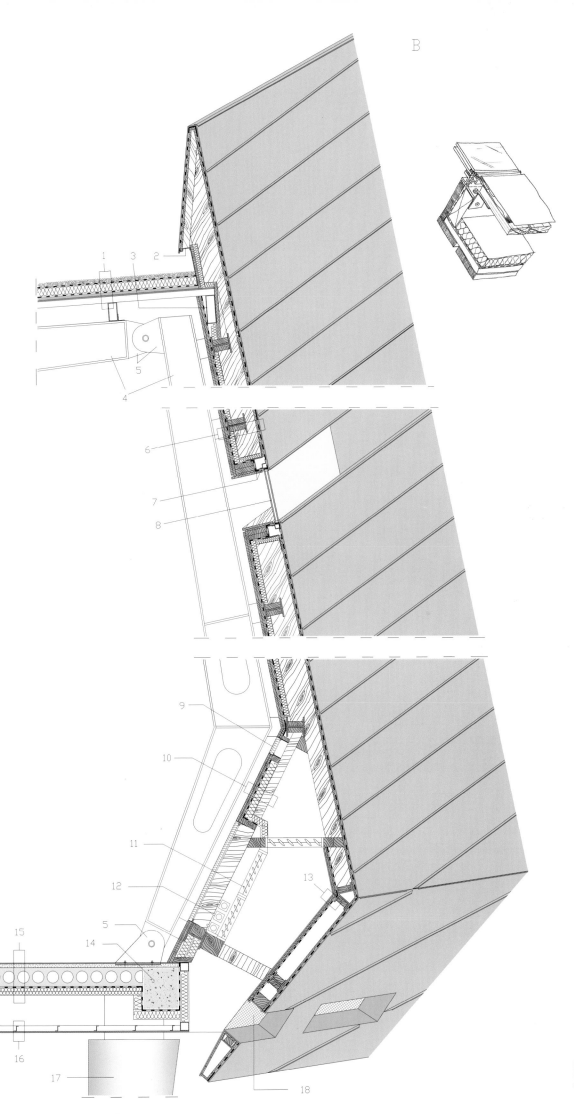

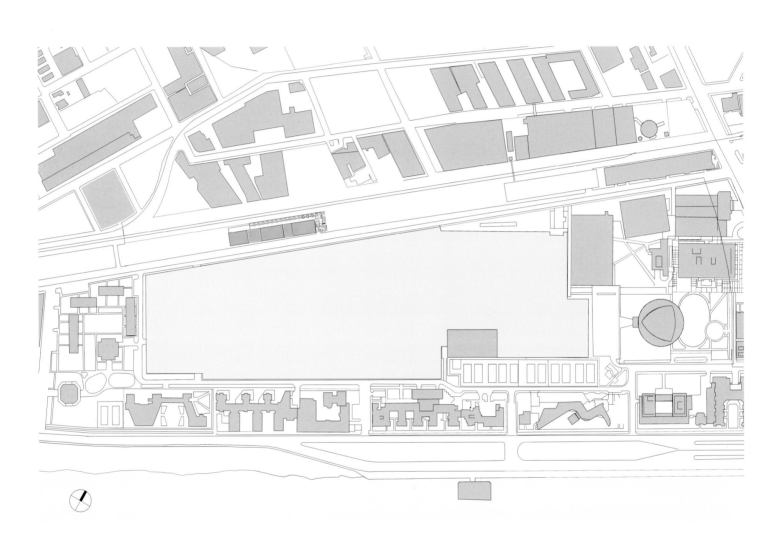

■ Site Plan – Scale 1:5000

At 380 ft (116 m) long, Simmons Hall was visualized as a vertical slice of a city and offers an alternative type of undergraduate living. The hall of residence at the Cambridge campus was conceived as one element of a strip of new MIT buildings along Vassar Street. Instead of the brick wall that is typical of urban Massachusetts, this strip was envisioned as a porous membrane made up of four or five different buildings in which light, materiality and transparency would be key.

Holl's central design concept for Simmons Hall was "porosity" – an idea that was inspired by a bath sponge. The façades of the ten-storey, 350-bed structure are wrapped in a matrix of square windows, the pores of the building. There are also a number of large-scale openings, which roughly correspond to main entrances, view corridors and principal outdoor terraces. The building's system of dynamic vertical cavities are its lungs, bringing natural light down and moving air up through the structure. Facilities include a 125-seat theatre, a night café, and a street-front restaurant with a special awning and outdoor tables. The 11-ft-wide (3 m) corridors connecting the rooms are like streets that happen upon urban experiences. As in Aalto's Baker House, also at MIT, the hallway is more like a public place, a lounge.

The dormitory residence is a special housing type that is not quite transient and not quite permanent. Social spaces must be planned to bring people together, provoking interaction, friendship and dialogue. At the same time, individuation of the students' rooms, the cluster or collective portion, and the overall residential buildings is also important in contributing to the vitality and identity of the residents. The urban planning of the residential dormitories should support their maximum potential as inspirational places to live and study. This is why individuals were given consideration over the mass population, so that each room would be a separate "house" with a particular identity.

The precast, steel-reinforced "PerfCon" concrete wall panels that make up the structure of Simmons Hall allow for maximum flexibility and interaction. The 18" (46 cm) depth of the wall naturally offers some protection from the heat of the summer sun, while letting in the low-angled winter light. Each of the dormitory's single rooms has nine operable windows over 2 x 2 ft (0.6 x 0.6 m) in size, giving students the choice between ventilating their rooms, simply enjoying the views or having some privacy. In the deep setting of the numerous windows, colour was applied to the head and jamb to create an identity for each of the ten "houses" within the overall building. The coloured jambs also show the anticipated maximum stresses in the structure. The colours correspond to the size of the reinforcing steel cast within the PerfCon panels (Blue = #5, Green = #6, Yellow = #7, Orange = #8, Red = #9 and #10, uncoloured areas are #5 or lower). Computer-generated structural models of the PerfCon structure showed areas that were critically overstressed due to long spans and bent spans over open corners. Selected windows in these areas were filled in to counter these effects.

With bedrock too deep to reach and soil too unstable to support friction piles, the building was designed to "float" like a boat in water. A volume of soil, equal to the weight of the building above, was excavated, so that once built, the pressure exerted by the building would equal the pressure from the soil that had been removed. A solid 4-ft-thick (1.2 m) concrete foundation evenly distributes the building load to the soil below.

■ Longitudinal Section – Scale 1:1000

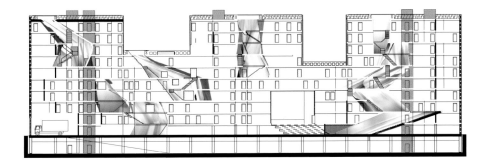

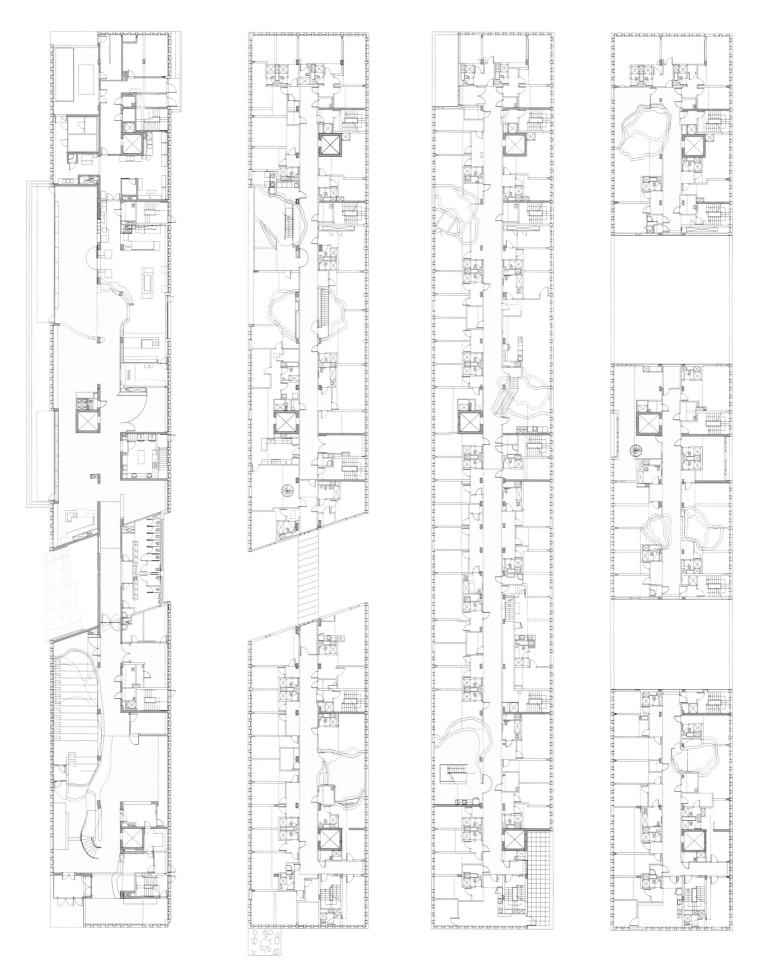

■ Ground Floor Plan – Scale 1:500　　　　■ Third Floor Plan – Scale 1:500　　　　■ Fifth Floor Plan – Scale 1:500　　　　■ Ninth Floor Plan – Scale 1:500

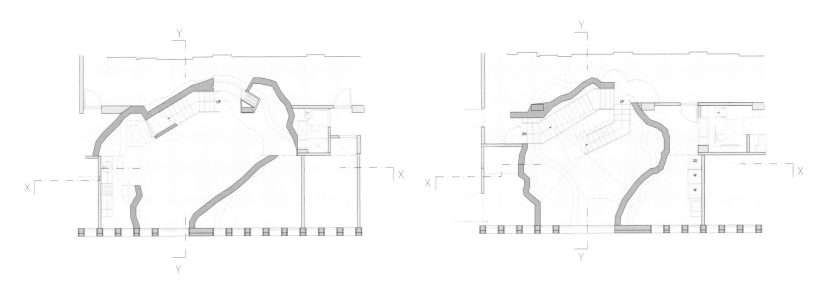

■ Seventh Floor Partial Plan – Scale 1:200

■ Eighth Floor Partial Plan – Scale 1:200

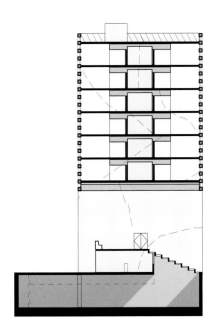

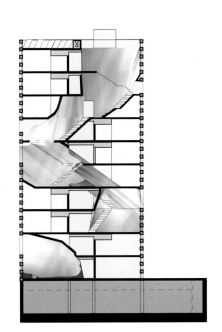

■ Cross Sections – Scale 1:500

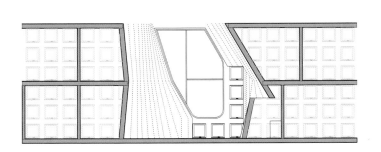

■ XX Section – Scale 1:200

■ YY Section – Scale 1:200

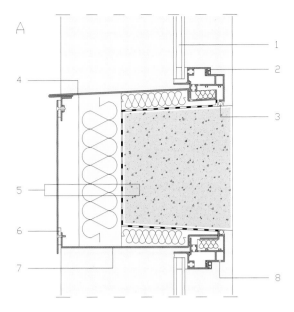

DETAILS A AND B: FAÇADE
VERTICAL AND HORIZONTAL SECTIONS
SCALE 1:10

1. Window with aluminium frame
   and insulating double glazing
2. Aluminium frame
   supporting fly screen
3. Backer rod and sealant
4. Folded sheet aluminium
   sill with hemmed edge
5. Aluminium panel cladding,
   air space, 4 1/2" (115 mm)
   board insulation, waterproofing
   membrane, reinforced
   concrete beam
6. Aluminium system
   securing infill panel
7. Sheet aluminium
8. Curtain track
9. Fixed corner angle panel
   of laminated glass in
   aluminium frame

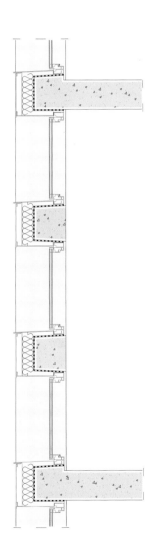

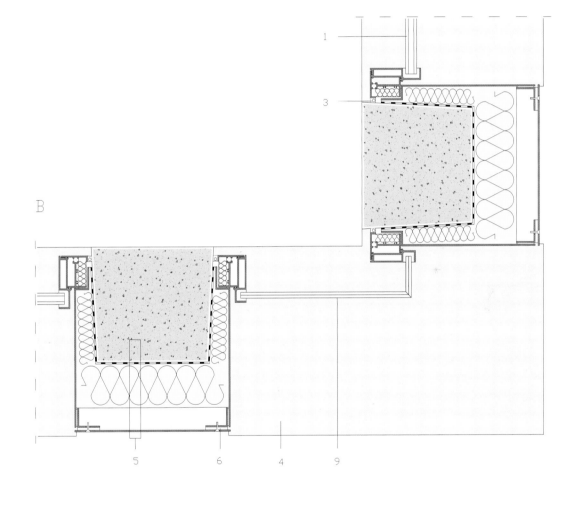

■ Detail – Vertical Section – Scale 1:30

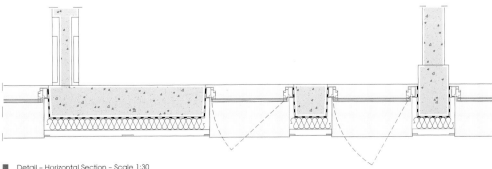

■ Detail – Horizontal Section – Scale 1:30

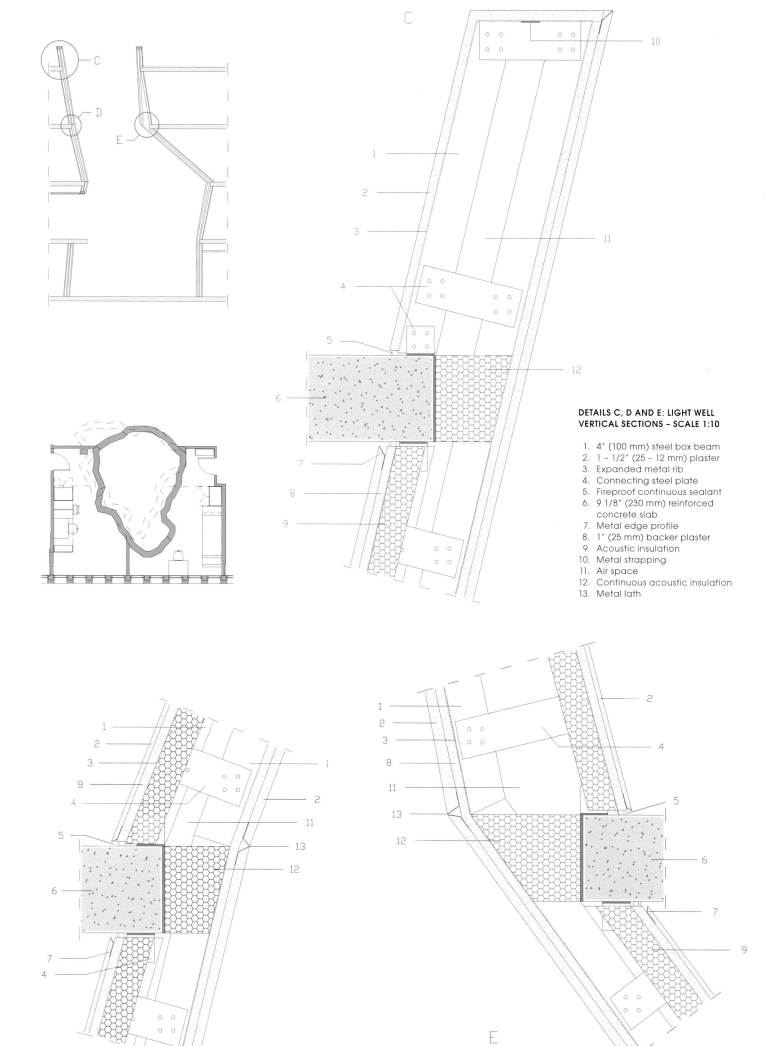

**DETAILS C, D AND E: LIGHT WELL
VERTICAL SECTIONS – SCALE 1:10**

1. 4" (100 mm) steel box beam
2. 1 - 1/2" (25 – 12 mm) plaster
3. Expanded metal rib
4. Connecting steel plate
5. Fireproof continuous sealant
6. 9 1/8" (230 mm) reinforced
   concrete slab
7. Metal edge profile
8. 1" (25 mm) backer plaster
9. Acoustic insulation
10. Metal strapping
11. Air space
12. Continuous acoustic insulation
13. Metal lath

RICHARD E. LINDNER ATHLETICS CENTER
UNIVERSITY OF CINCINNATI, USA

BERNARD TSCHUMI ARCHITECTS

The new Lindner sports centre designed by Bernard Tschumi covers an area of 258,000 ft² (24,000 m²); of its eight storeys, three are below ground level. The building links the south and north entrances to the university campus and provides a fulcrum for the whole Richard E. Lindner Varsity Village with its prominent three stadiums: the Marge Schott, the Nippert and the Gettler.

The broad central hallway opens all the way up to the great glass skylight. These impressive dimensions make it the heart of all campus sports events, a meeting ground for students, trainers and university staff. Four of its five flanking storeys are occupied by graphics for the George and Helen Smith Athletics Museum, designed by Eva Maddox from Chicago. A 20 ft (6 m) screen in this museum shows short videos on the history of all sports. The multi-storey hall and the ranks of museum display cases are what catches the eye as one first enters this building, with its deliberate use of depth and full natural lighting from the glass ceiling.

The north-south monumental red stairway "floats" down the centre of the hallway, linking the basements to the eighth storey. It hovers in thin air, resting on horizontal bars at either end and with no other visible support below. The upper floors house offices, an auditorium, the museum, shops, a gym for training, and sports medical and first-aid services; the basements contain changing rooms and technical plant. The project was subject to one constraint in the form of a pre-existing underground utility space which had to be kept free of pillars and was needed for access to the loading platforms of adjacent buildings.

To ensure unbroken spans, the structural system devised is a rigid trellis-like perimeter, an outer skeleton in the form of a steel triangular-shaped lattice, in which the columns slant upwards diagonally close to one another, joining into one continuous truss that covers the whole space below.

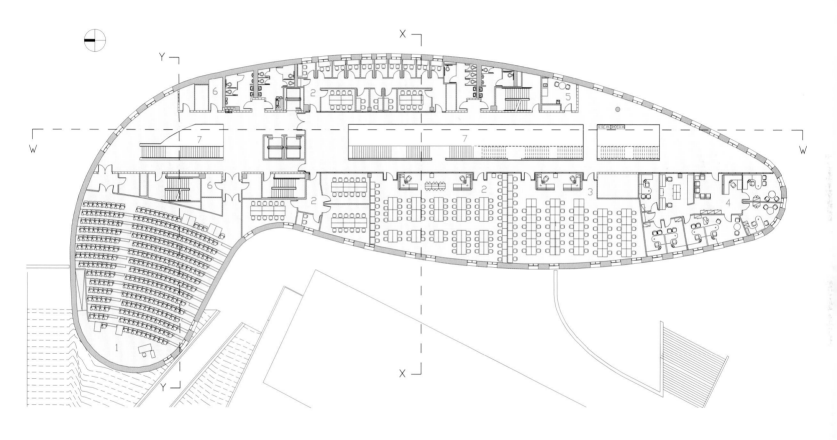

■ Fifth Floor Plan – Scale 1:500

1. Lecture hall
2. Study room
3. Computer laboratory
4. Office
5. Shared copy and break room
6. Technical room
7. Atrium

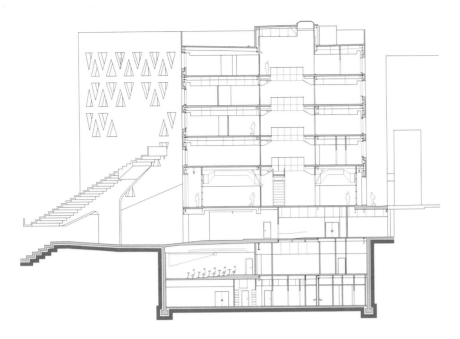

■ XX Cross Section – Scale 1:500

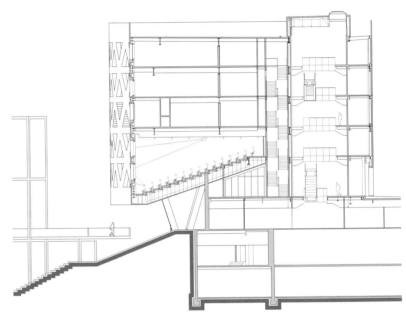

■ YY Cross Section – Scale 1:500

■ WW Longitudinal Section – Scale 1:500

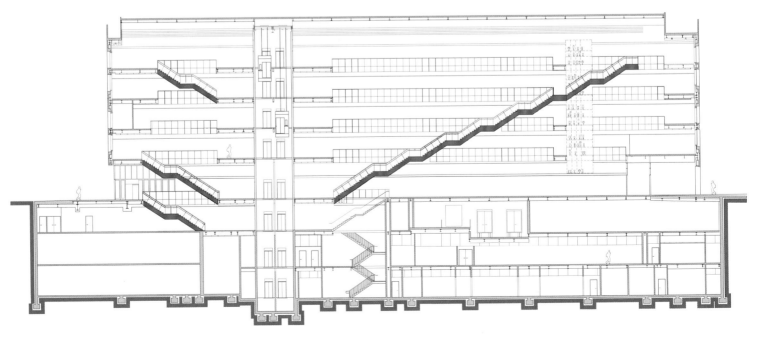

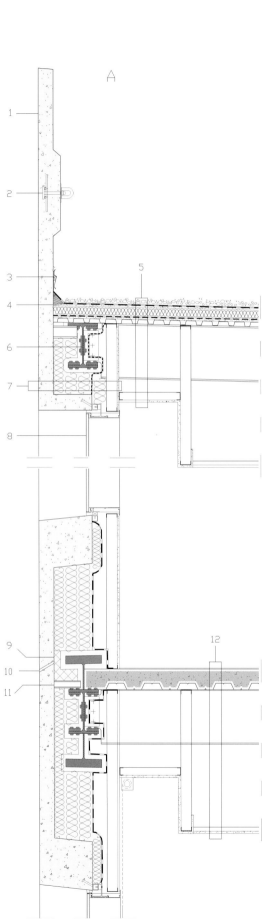

A

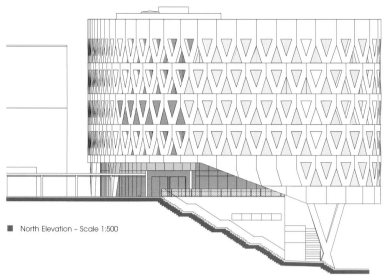

**DETAIL A: EAST FAÇADE
VERTICAL SECTION – SCALE 1:30**

1. Superstructure in 4 5/8" (120 mm) thick pre-cast concrete panels
2. Bolted and welded stainless steel anchors
3. Elastomeric flashing
4. Wood fibre angle support for flashing
5. Ballast layer, waterproofing membrane, glued 3/8" (10 mm) gypsum board panels, 3" (75 mm) double insulation layer, vapour barrier, glued 3/8" (10 mm) gypsum board panels, 1 3/8" (35 mm) corrugated sheeting, spray-on fireproof insulation, 17" (430 mm) H double T-section steel joist, suspended ceiling on frame formed by steel box-shaped profiles
6. 13 3/4" (350 mm) H double T-section steel joist protected by fireproof insulation
7. Cladding in 4 5/8" (120 mm) pre-cast concrete panels, expanded polystyrene insulation finished in fibreglass, fireproof sealant, insulation filling, suspended ceiling structure in steel box-shaped profiles
8. Triangular aluminium frames with 1/4 – 1/2 – 1/4" (6 – 12 – 6 mm) double glazing
9. Mineral wool insulation filling
10. 3/4" (20 mm) thick panel joints
11. Steel bar securing concrete cladding
12. Carpeting, floor formed by concrete fill over 2" (50 mm) corrugated sheeting, 17" (430 mm) H double T-section steel joist, suspended ceiling in acoustic insulation panels on frame in steel box-shaped profiles
13. Suspended ceiling in gypsum board panels with waterproof finish, 5 7/8" (150 mm) board insulation
14. Steel angle profiles attached to lower edge of joist to support curtain wall
15. Metal louvres for ventilation, air space, metal slats
16. Insulated metal ventilated shaft
17. 4" (100 mm) smooth concrete screed, rigid waterproofing membrane, concrete screed forming variable slope, 6 1/4" (160 mm) reinforced concrete slab
18. Downspout for rainwater
19. Metal profiles connecting suspended ceiling to joist

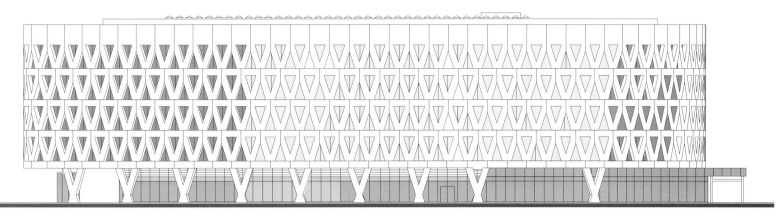

■ East Elevation – Scale 1:500

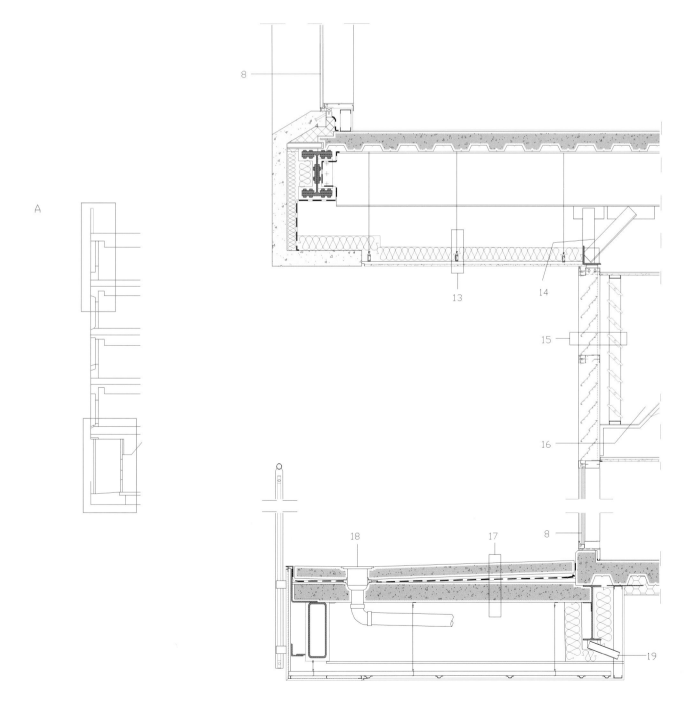

A

8

13

14

15

16

18

17

8

19

DETAILS B AND C:
VERTICAL SECTIONS OF V-SHAPED
COLUMNS – SCALE 1:50

1. Spandrel cladding in pre-cast concrete panels
2. Mineral wool insulation layer
3. 5 7/8" (150 mm) H double T-section steel joist with fireproof insulation and bolted reinforcing plates
4. Expanded polystyrene insulation finished in fibreglass
5. V-shaped column cladding in pre-cast concrete panels, double T-section steel joist forming diagonal structural grating, spray-on fireproof insulation
6. Concrete screed, double high-density board insulation with drainage channels, waterproofing membrane, screed, sloping drainage layer, floor formed by concrete fill over corrugated sheeting, 15 3/4" (400 mm) double T-section steel joist
7. Waterproofing membrane
8. Suspended ceiling in gypsum board panels with waterproofing finish, 5 7/8" (150 mm) board insulation
9. Metal louvres for ventilation, air space, insulating metal slats
10. Metal profiles connecting suspended ceiling to joist
11. Cavity wall in 4" (100 mm) brick, air space, metal wall ties positioned every 15 3/4" (400 mm), 2" (50 mm) board insulation,
12. 7 7/8" (200 mm) perforated brick wall with mortar fill
13. 17 3/4" (450 mm) H double T-section steel joist protected by fireproof insulation
14. 26 3/4" (680 mm) H double T-section steel joist protected by fireproof insulation
15. 1/2" (12 mm) concrete screed, 2" (50 mm) floor formed by concrete fill over corrugated sheeting, 9 7/8" (250 mm) H double T-section steel joist

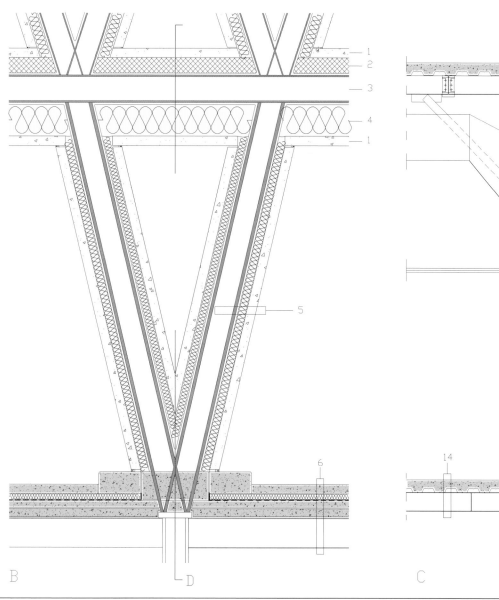

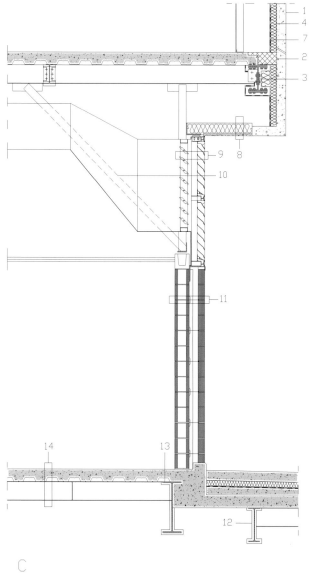

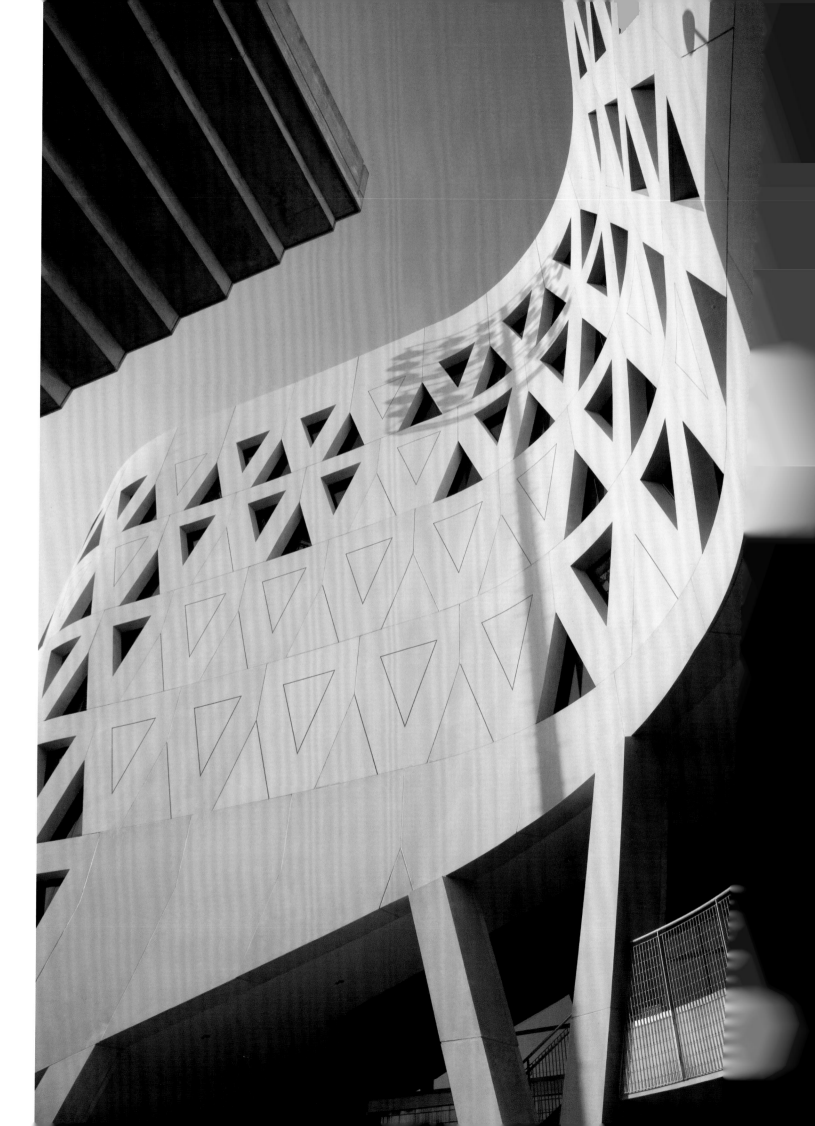

CAMPUS RECREATION CENTER
UNIVERSITY OF CINCINNATI, USA
MORPHOSIS / THOM MAYNE

The new Recreation Center of the University of Cincinnati (UCR) is a multi-purpose facility, designed as a point of cohesion and interchange. With its sports complex, reading room, covered refreshment areas, canteen, dormitories and student accommodation, this Morphosis venture – with participation by local KZF Design – forms part of the scheme to transform the university campus into a continuously used hub of vitality in line with the master plan conceived by landscape architect George Hargreaves in 1989. The Recreation Center is a crossroads for the whole campus. It stands on Main Street, forming a connector with surrounding buildings and itself wrapping around the football stadium.

Being on the main campus thoroughfare, it is a focal point for all lesser routes and a landmark/vantage point, as well as symbolically epitomizing the polyhedric university experience. In placing the Recreation Center within the true Morphosis design tradition – "a stand … against uniformity" – Thom Mayne offers a clue to our interpretation: variety of form and function is the essence of this project. The complex extends over 355,000 ft^2 (33,000 m^2) and rises to 52 ft (16 m) in height.

There is an organic quality about the curving, undulating roof, dotted with skylights, which holds together the whole Center: the gymnasium with its six basket- and volley-ball courts, the water garden, restaurant and cafeteria, the fitness centre and other points of recreation. The main body is a dog-legged cube, clad in aluminium slats and formed of cell-like residential units. A curving wing veiled in pierced metal houses the teaching section. The two buildings stand facing one another against the backdrop of the park.

■ Ground Floor Plan – Scale 1:1000

1. Recreation pool
2. Storage
3. Lap pool
4. Office
5. Gymnasium
6. Corridor
7. Locker room
8. Classroom
9. Housing

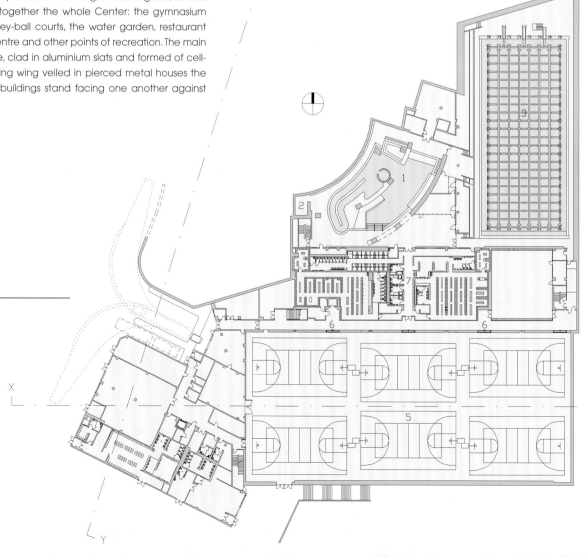

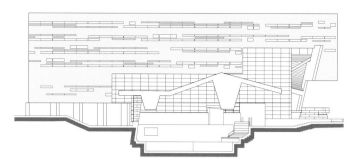

■ North Elevation – Scale 1:1000

206 / Recreation Center

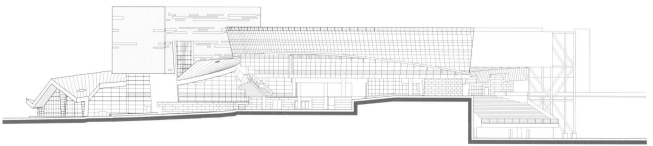

■ East Elevation – Scale 1:1000

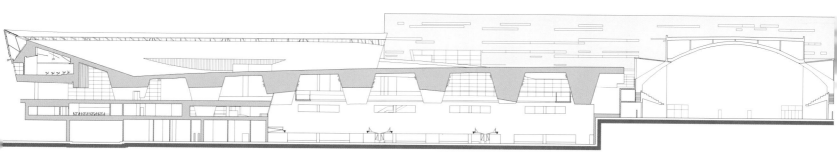

■ XX Section – Scale 1:1000

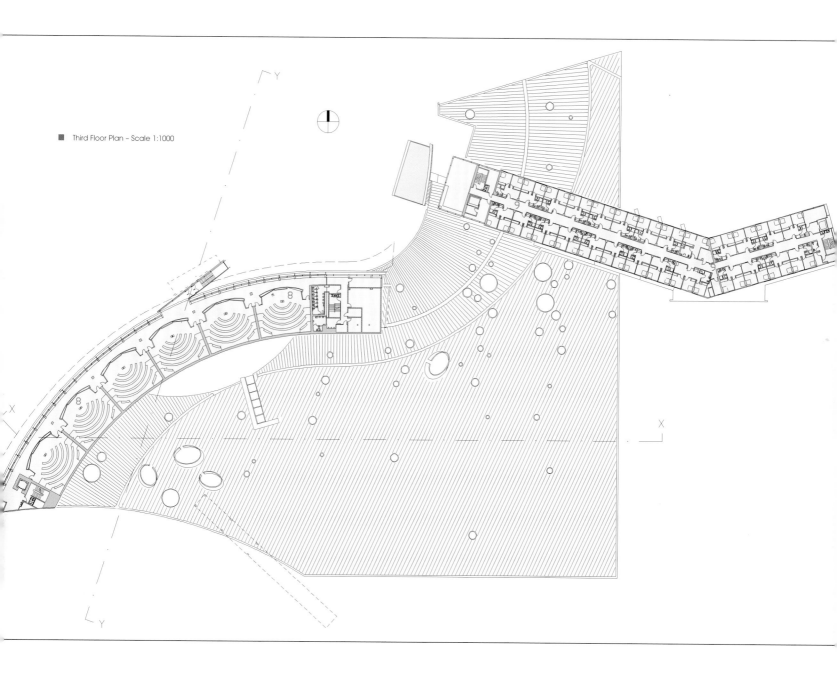

■ Third Floor Plan – Scale 1:1000

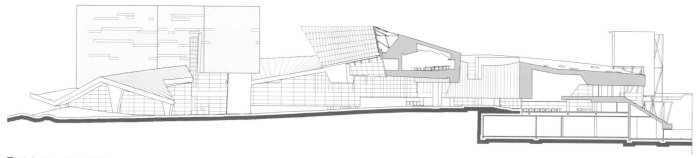

■ YY Section – Scale 1:1000

DETAIL A: DWELLINGS
VERTICAL SECTION – SCALE 1:40

1. Aluminium flashing
    with wood fastener
2. Ballast, asphalt membrane,
    waterproofing panel of varying
    thickness to form slope,
    1 5/8" (40 mm) corrugated
    sheeting, 4" (100 mm) steel purlin,
    9 7/8" (250 mm) H steel double
    T-section principal girder
3. Lighting with shading recessed
    in suspended ceiling
4. Suspended ceiling in 5/8" (16 mm)
    thick gypsum board panels

on framework of
3 1/2" (90 mm) steel profiles
5. Aluminium double-glazing
    assembly with 1/4 – 1/2 – 1/4"
    (6 – 12 – 6 mm) glazing
6. Cladding in 2" (50 mm)
    insulating metal panels fastened
    to 4" (100 mm) steel frame,
    internal cladding in 5/8" (16 mm)
    thick gypsum board panels
7. 3 1/8" (80 mm) reinforced concrete
    slab with honed stone flooring,
    2 3/4" (70 mm) corrugated
    sheeting, 7 7/8" (200 mm)
    steel double T-section girder,
    suspended ceiling in

5/8" (16 mm) thick gypsum
board panels supported
by metal tie rod structure
8. Semi-rigid insulation between
    metal panels and slab
9. Ballast, asphalt membrane,
    waterproofing panel,
    3 1/8" (80 mm) reinforced
    concrete, 3" (75 mm) corrugated
    sheeting, 7 7/8" (200 mm) H steel
    double T-section girder
10. Cladding in 5 7/8" (150 mm)
    thick pre-cast concrete panels
    supported by horizontal steel
    box-shaped profiles, 7 7/8"
    (200 mm) steel column

of principal structure,
2 1/2" (60 mm) board
insulation, framework of
steel box-shaped profiles
supporting 5/8" (16 mm)
gypsum board panels
11. Suspended ceiling in
    7/8" (23 mm) laminated
    wood panels on
    5 7/8" (150 mm) steel purlins
12. 2 3/8" (65 mm) solid wood
    flooring, 3 1/8" (80 mm)
    reinforced concrete slab,
    3" (75 mm) corrugated sheeting
13. 13 3/4" (350 mm) H steel
    double T-section girder

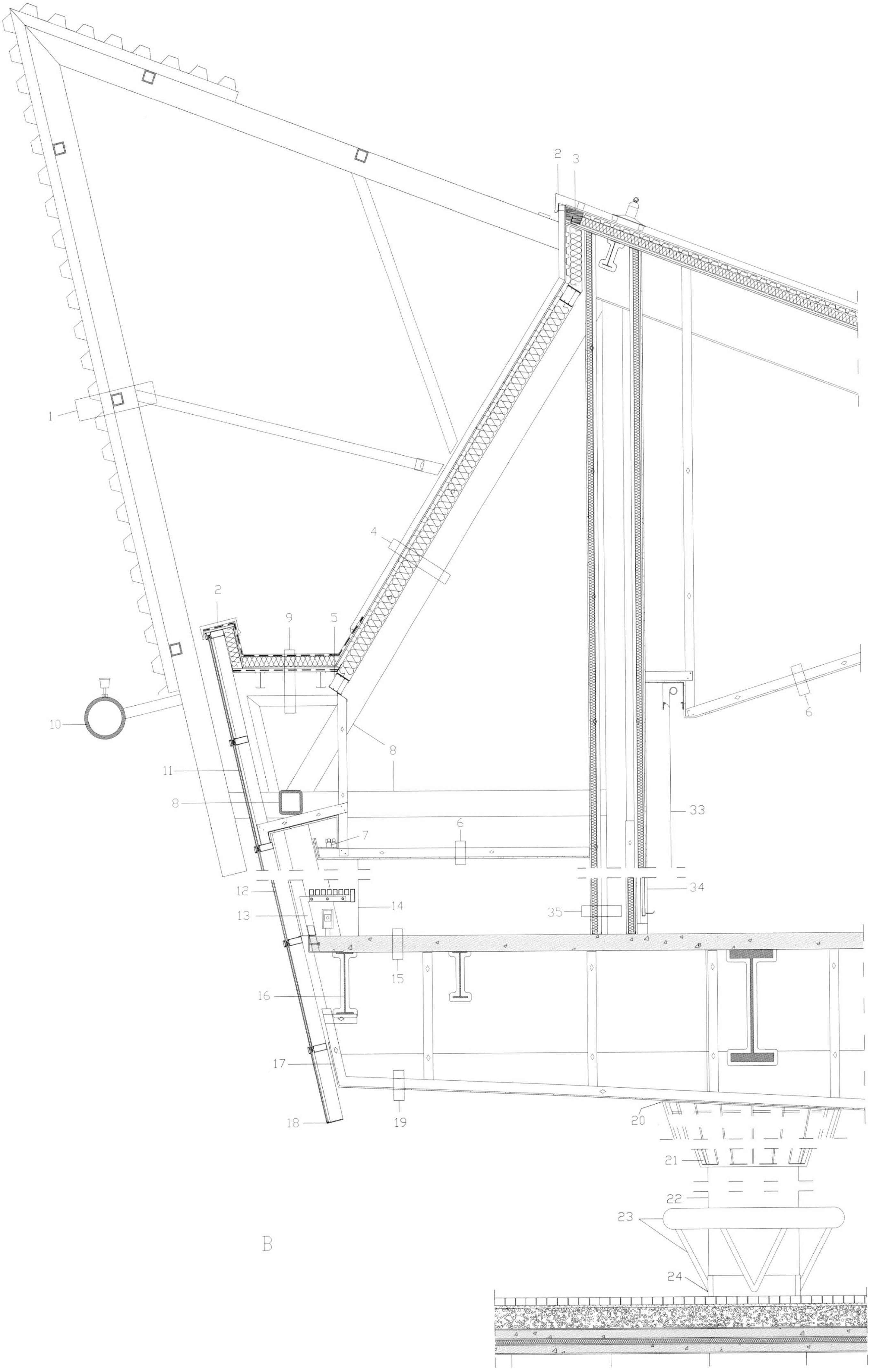

1

2
3

2

4

9
5

10

11

8

7

12
13

14

15

16

17

18   19

B

6

33

34
35

20

21

22

23

24

DETAIL B: TRANSVERSE SECTION OF CLASSROOM BUILDING – SCALE 1:50

1. Microperforated sheet metal sun shading supported by principal and secondary structures in painted galvanized steel box-shaped profiles
2. Flashing
3. Fireproof wood battens supporting flashing
4. Cladding in 2 1/2" (60 mm) metal panels, 5/8" (16 mm) gypsum board panel, 1 5/8" (42 mm) corrugated sheeting, 6 1/4" (160 mm) board insulation, 10 5/8" (270 mm) H steel box-shaped girder
5. Steel box-shaped profiles nailed to principal structure, supporting suspended ceiling
6. Suspended ceiling in 5/8" (16 mm) gypsum board panels supported by metal profile framework
7. Lighting system with fluorescent tubes recessed in suspended ceiling
8. Load-bearing structure in welded 10 5/8" (270 mm) H steel box-shaped girders
9. Waterproofing membrane, 4" (100 mm) double layer of extruded polystyrene insulation, 1 3/8" (35 mm) corrugated sheeting, vapour barrier, 6 1/4" (160 mm) H double C-section steel joist, wind-bracing frame in 4" (100 mm) thick steel tubular profiles
10. Steel tubular profiles anchored to principal structure with supports for fixing lights
11. Insulated opaque glass infill panel
12. Structural glass wall with silicone joints and 1/4 – 1/2 – 1/4 (6 – 12 – 6 mm) double glazing in 7 7/8" (200 mm) thick aluminium frames
13. Aluminium bench with radiator underneath
14. Aluminium column finished with Kynar sheeting
15. 6 3/4" (170 mm) reinforced concrete floor with honed stone flooring
16. Double T-section steel girders of various heights supporting floor
17. Upturned section of insulated suspended ceiling with neoprene sealant
18. Structure closing off lower part of glazed wall formed by C-section profile welded to aluminium plate
19. Suspended ceiling in 5/8" (16 mm) thick gypsum board panels with board insulation, supported by frame in steel box-shaped profiles
20. Watertight joint between capital and suspended ceiling
21. Capital finished with double layer of gypsum board on sheet metal grid
22. 39 3/8" (1000 mm) Ø reinforced concrete column
23. Column base fitted with structure in welded and painted galvanized steel tubular profiles with diameters of 7 7/8" (200 mm) and 2" (50 mm)
24. Pair of 3/8" (10 mm) thick painted galvanized steel plates bolted to column
25. Flooring in 3 1/8" (80 mm) square concrete blocks, 1" (25 mm) cement mortar topping, 7 7/8" (200 mm) ballast filling, 4 1/2" (115 mm) reinforced concrete slab, 1 3/4" (45 mm) high-density board insulation, 3 1/8" (80 mm) reinforced concrete slab with waterproofing membrane
26. 5/8" (16 mm) thick gypsum board panels supported by frame of steel box-shaped profiles, 16 1/2" (420 mm) reinforced concrete wall, 2" (50 mm) acoustic board, reinforced concrete wall
27. External cladding in 1 3/8" (35 mm) metal sheeting anchored to omega-section metal profiles, 5/8" (16 mm) thick gypsum board panels supported by frame of steel box-shaped profiles
28. Lighting recess in suspended ceiling screened by etched acrylic panels
29. Suspended concrete platform with honed stone finish and rounded edges
30. Desks fixed to floor
31. Metal ventilation grid
32. Projector
33. Motorized projector screen recessed into suspended ceiling
34. Blackboard with fixed or sliding panel
35. Partition in 5/8" (16 mm) thick gypsum board, fibreglass board insulation, frame in 4" (100 mm) steel profiles, 7 7/8" (200 mm) steel double T-section column

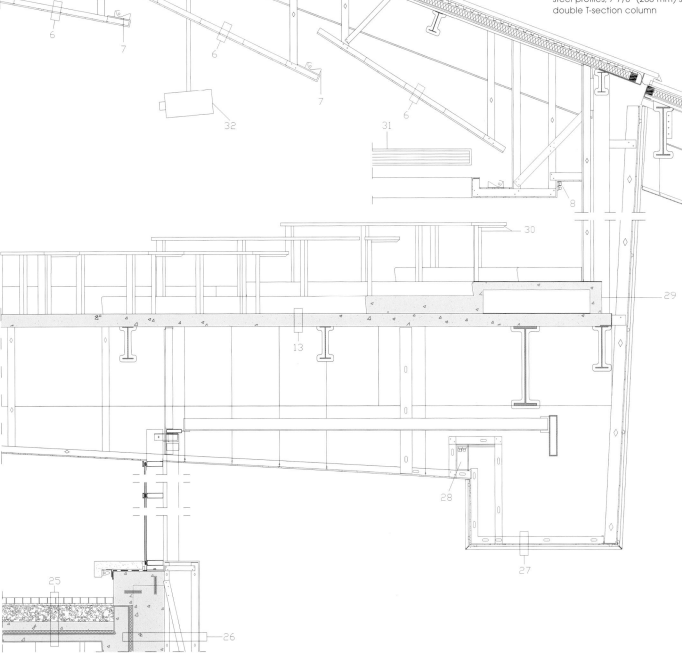

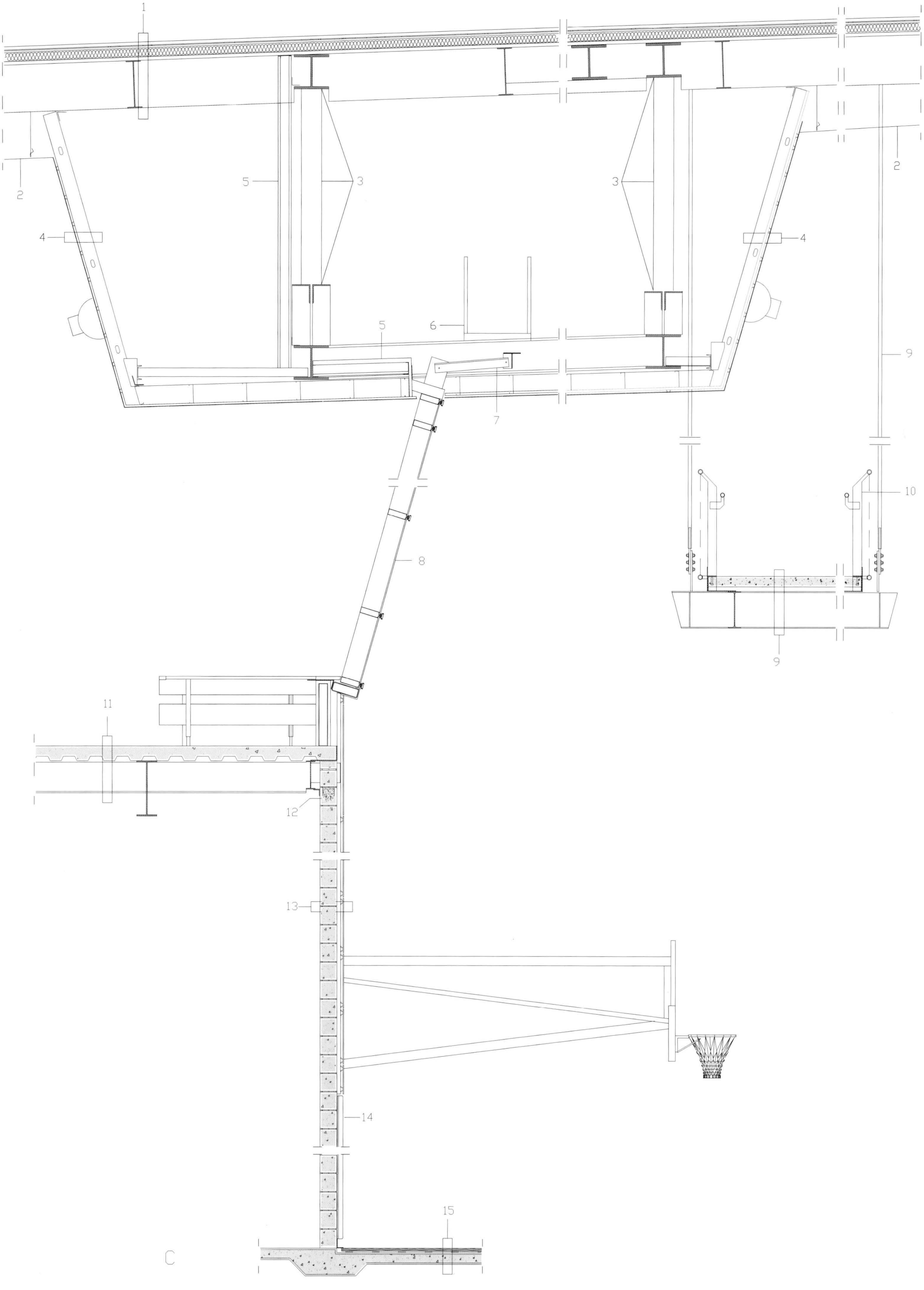
1
2
5
3
3
4
4
2
5
6
9
7
10
8
9
11
12
13
14
15
C

DETAIL C: GYMNASIUM
VERTICAL SECTION – SCALE 1:50

1. 1 3/8" (35 mm) metal panel cladding, 5/8" (16 mm) thick gypsum board panel, 4" (100 mm) waterproofing panel, 1 5/8" (40 mm) corrugated sheeting, 21 1/4" (540 mm) H double T-section girder
2. Steel grating false ceiling suspended by steel tie rods fixed to load-bearing structure
3. Trussed structure formed by 15" (380 mm) H steel double T-section girders,

9 1/2" (240 mm) H steel uprights and crosspieces formed by connected 7 7/8" (200 mm) H L-section angle profiles
4. Trussed structure cladding in aluminium panels on steel omega-profiles fixed to steel box-shaped profiles
5. 6 1/4" (160 mm) thick fire-resistant wall
6. Maintenance walkway
7. Pair of 4" (100 mm) steel L-profiles supporting glazed wall
8. 1/2" (12 mm) thick glazed wall with 9 7/8" (250 mm) thick aluminium frame

9. Ring suspended on steel tie rod formed by 4 5/8" (120 mm) concrete slab with acrylic resin finish, 2" (50 mm) corrugated sheeting, structure in 16 1/2" (420 mm) H steel girders
10. Handrail fixed to steel uprights and metal grille parapet
11. 4 5/8" (120 mm) reinforced concrete slab with honed stone flooring, 2" (50 mm) corrugated sheeting, 9 7/8" (250 mm) steel double T-section girder
12. Reinforced concrete spandrel

with metal L-profiles nailed to interior face providing additional support to principal steel girder
13. Wall in 7 7/8" (200 mm) concrete blocks, framework of steel uprights and crosspieces supporting fibreglass-reinforced concrete panels
14. Fireproof foam rubber with vinyl resin finish on 1/2" (12 mm) plywood panels, mounted on metal Z-profile stirrups
15. Painted wood parquetry flooring on shock absorption pads, 5 1/8" (130 mm) reinforced concrete slab

OMA's new concert hall in Porto, the Casa da Música – a faceted concrete structure that cost 75 m Euros to build – opened on 14 April 2005 just off the Rotunda da Boavista, a large roundabout in a plaza near the city centre. To mark the occasion, there were no fewer than twenty-six performances by singers and musicians across the entire musical spectrum, using all the spaces in the 237,000 ft² (22,000 m²) building – its 1,200- and 350-seat auditoria, teaching spaces, cyber music and multimedia production area, rehearsal and workshop spaces, restaurant, bars and shops. When Porto was selected as a European Capital of Culture in 2001, the Ministry of Culture and the City Council established Porto 2001, an organization to create new urban and cultural initiatives.

The Casa da Música was one such initiative and OMA was the architectural practice of choice. Epic, exuberant and sensuously beautiful, the design actually evolved from a concept for a house. Rather than appealing solely to a specific concert-going public, the building aims to address the city as a whole. The solitary form punctuated by big windows, and adjoining the historic park of the Rotunda da Boavista, is fronted by a steep flight of steps in concrete with a ribbed aluminium finish, rising to a huge sliding recessed door. Below the plaza are three levels that contain 600 parking places.

The building's presence mediates a fresh relationship between new and old models of the city by means of windows exposing functions across boundaries: the auditorium box opened up via entirely glazed corrugated glass front and back walls, a plural trajectory of stairs, platforms and escalators connecting circulation space with the secondary spaces of foyers, a restaurant, bars and a terrace, and the city beyond. Accommodating extensive rehearsal and soloist spaces and dressing rooms for the Porto Philharmonic Orchestra and guest performers, the building's 16" (40 cm) thick faceted shell and the two 3-ft-thick (1 m) walls of the main auditorium form the key load-carrying and stability system. OMA researched new applications and materials: the concrete mix, corrugated glass that looks like curtains, antique tiles sourced locally and the auditorium wall finish. The late furniture designer Maarten van Severen designed the single block of adjustable auditorium seating in grey-silver wool velvet with LED armrest lighting, which creates a sparkling field of light. Works by Daciano da Costa, a veteran Portuguese furniture designer who collaborated with Niemeyer, over a forty-year career, were newly produced to create public seating. Interior designer Petra Blaisse created eleven curtains in colourless fishnet, voile and velvet, and initiated the idea for the gold-leaf finish on the auditorium walls.

The effect of experimentation for strictly functional purposes creates a highly cohesive, articulate expression of a new vision for plural contemporary urban space.

■ Site Plan – Scale 1:3500

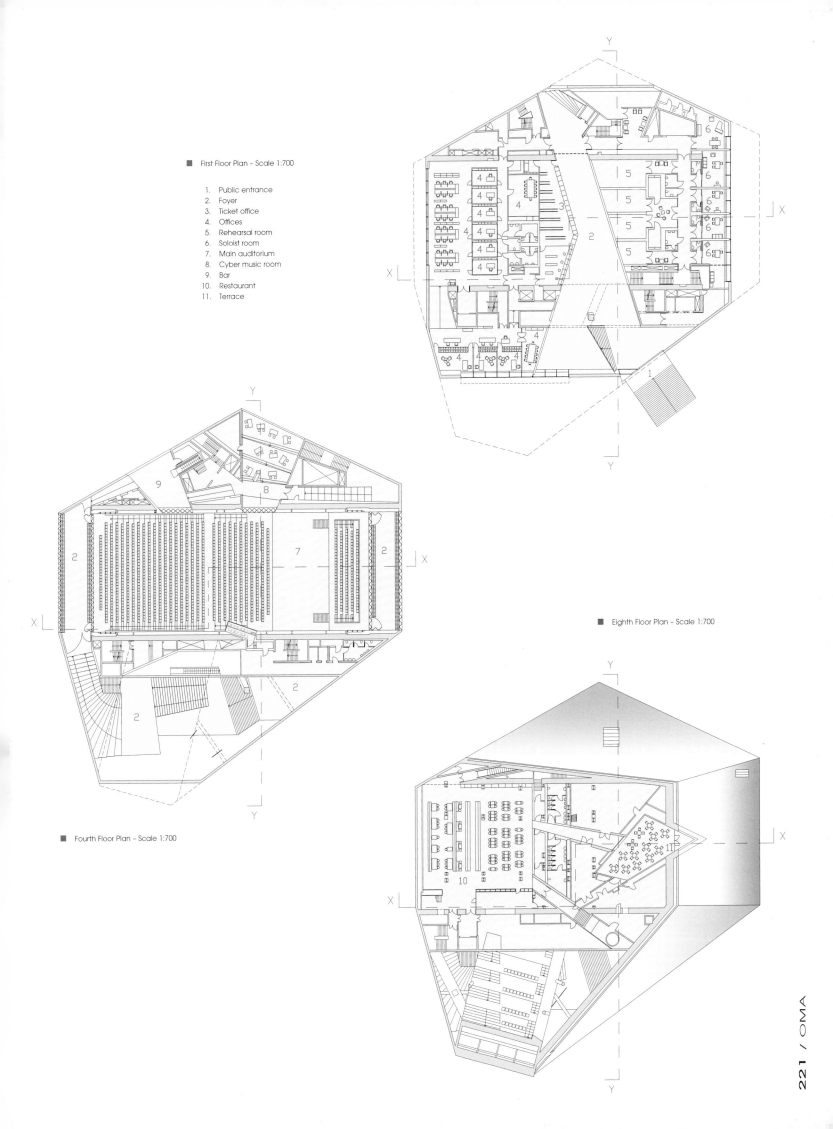

■ First Floor Plan – Scale 1:700

1. Public entrance
2. Foyer
3. Ticket office
4. Offices
5. Rehearsal room
6. Soloist room
7. Main auditorium
8. Cyber music room
9. Bar
10. Restaurant
11. Terrace

■ Fourth Floor Plan – Scale 1:700

■ Eighth Floor Plan – Scale 1:700

221 / OMA

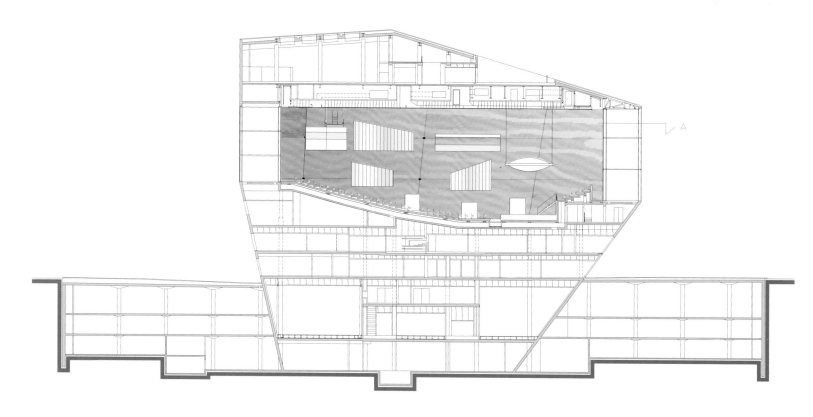

■ XX Section – Scale 1:600

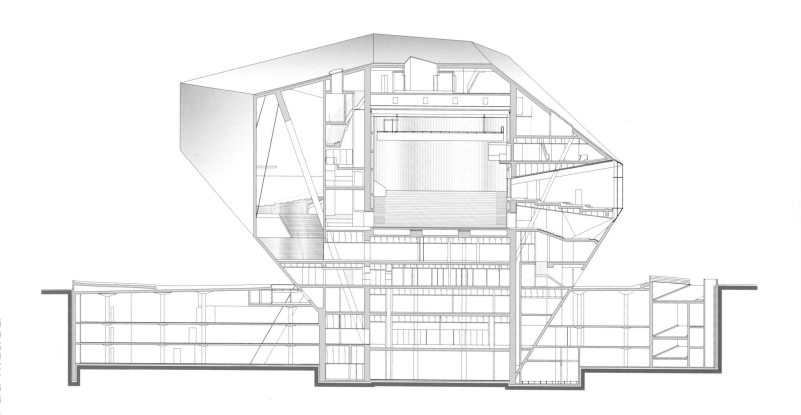

■ YY Section – Scale 1:600

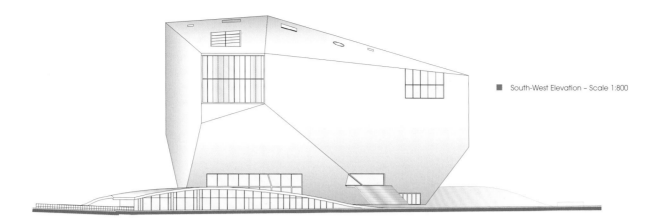

■ South-West Elevation – Scale 1:800

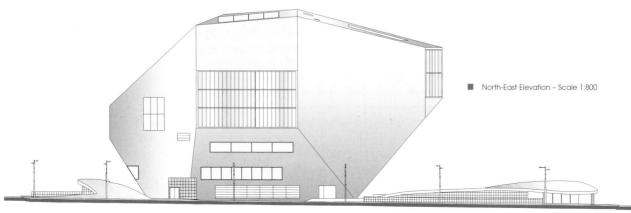

■ North-East Elevation – Scale 1:800

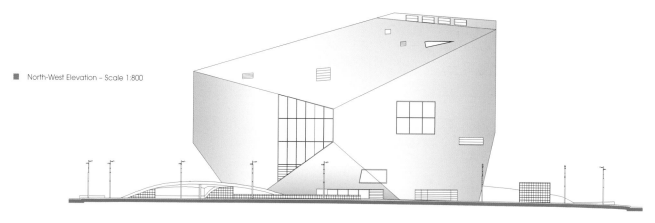

■ North-West Elevation – Scale 1:800

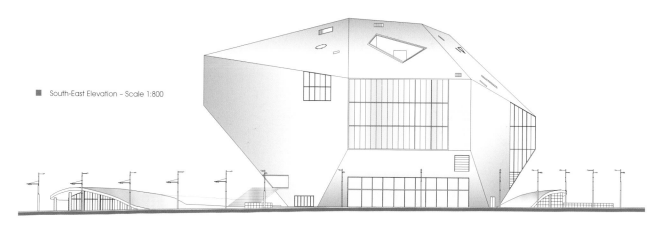

■ South-East Elevation – Scale 1:800

INTERVIEW WITH ELLEN VAN LOON

BY LUCY BULLIVANT

Lucy Bullivant - Can you explain the concept for the building? It seems the antithesis of an orthodox monocultural concert hall. The treatment of the spaces around the two auditoria is highly significant: there is the sense of a generative public architecture supportive of difference, an exploratory journey where circulation and function become mutually informing, isn't there? At the same time, Rem has reportedly said that in the building nothing is entirely visual; everything is integrated as part of the way the building works, and then becomes aesthetic.

Ellen van Loon - We took the classical 'shoe box' of an auditorium and changed its experience by puncturing it with windows on each side, providing views of the city. All the leftover space is a vertical loop of circulation space with rooms of various functions along with way that spins through the building. On the south side a very high foyer opens up with stairs rising; they rake around to the right in between the escalators to the smaller auditorium. On the north side we introduce a tunnel concept, with lots of connecting floors.

The client wanted to have a building that accommodated festivals as well as several types of individual performances at the same time. We combined the notion of processional space and a musical loop, and gave the option to have audio connections in all the foyers. The building can then accommodate small as well as large events – everything from the classical Orchestra Gulbenkian, Alfred Brendel piano concerts, to world music, jazz, electronica and techno festivals and a foyer that is a bar, using circulation space that otherwise would be dead space. It's a bit like an instrument. We addressed the relationship between the building, its public, the plaza on which it sits and the wider city by regarding it as a solid mass from which are eliminated two concert halls and all the other public spaces. This creates a hollowed-out block so the building can reveal its contents to the city.

L.B. - You are lucky that the programme for the building you were commissioned to design is so inspired: whose idea was it?

E.v.L. - The original idea for the building as a house of music that is a multidisciplinary platform for all its forms came from Pedro Burmester, a famous pianist from Porto, who was on the Board of Directors until 2002.

L.B. - The concept for the Casa da Música was developed from one OMA made six years ago for a villa for a seemingly aloof family in which each member would have open yet isolated spaces, wasn't it? Similarly the Casa design is geared towards being constantly open to the public, creating what Rem calls 'a live infrastructure' that also demystifies the activities of professional musicians and stimulates a closer relationship between public and artistes.

E.v.L. - We try out new concepts for buildings to see how they might work spatially. A Dutch client wanted a house; he didn't like his family much so it was to be one with a lot of personal space. We centred it on a main living room like a shoebox, with a lot of storage space around it. Then we thought, as this project had not gone ahead, why don't we use the concept as a theoretical model for the Porto project, and group rooms around the auditorium. The villa was scaled up five times. We designed it on paper with the model next to us, and as we went along we discovered areas – like the roof-space that in the later stages became a meeting and relaxation space and an observatory with a sloped ceiling and half retractable glass roof that allows you to emerge to roof height and see panoramic views of the city. However many experiments you do with the model, it is only when it is on site that you really feel how the architecture is.

L.B. - The building, a bold diamond shape, looks relatively austere due to its concrete surface, set against the warm glow of the plaza travertine while the interior has stimulating episodes of colours and textures. Frequently throughout, its materiality refers to its cultural context, and the plainness of the exterior lets the urban setting have its place. What the priorities informed your choices?

E.v.L. - The exterior is white, self-compacting concrete, faceted as we planned from the very beginning. Portugal is one of the few countries where you can do beautiful concrete and people are used to craftwork in this field. We had many tests done because the mix often used in the country is limestone and white cement, but sometimes that produces a yellowish gluey appearance, so we used grey granite sand and white cement.

The Portuguese tiles that you see lining the VIP rooms and roof terrace are not meant to be ironic, we love the tradition. They add a sense of fun and are beautiful. The black and white pattern on the roof terrace refers, according to local rumours, to the colours of the Boavista football team; then we have Italian Renaissance tiles in green and white, and Delft blue tiles inside the VIP room. We worked with a Spanish glass manufacturer on the corrugated glass that we use on the auditorium windows. In the auditorium we wanted natural wood walls but patterning on top was not feasible, so we enlarged the wood pattern with a gold leaf abstract.

The cyber music room where the public can interact to play electronic music is lined with walls of bright green epoxy paint on rubber. There's a purple-fabric-clad room overlooking the auditorium for kids, with sloping floors and rubber-clad walls for drawings. The plaza itself is gold travertine marble, 97,000 ft² (9,000 m²) of it, so we sourced it from Jordan to keep the costs under control. We wanted to have this very warm colour. Overall we tried not to have too big a palette of materials, but just as you have a sense of varied circulation, you find differences in materials.

L.B. - Rem is well known for his polemics about context, and he recently talked of the potential of "a building as a contextual machine", which interests me greatly from the perspective of generating new urban conditions from the inside out. Now that you can see the result of your five-year project, how do you interpret its contextual value?

E.v.L. - For us, context means the relationship of the building to the people and life of the city, and by opening up views and designing internal spaces as we have, the public can easily access this new environment. Many of the competition entries featured the concert hall as a block, but we felt it needed active space around it too as well as inside it. Within the first few weeks the plaza is already being used daily for skating, biking and capoeira, it's really working.

SALA1 II-VII

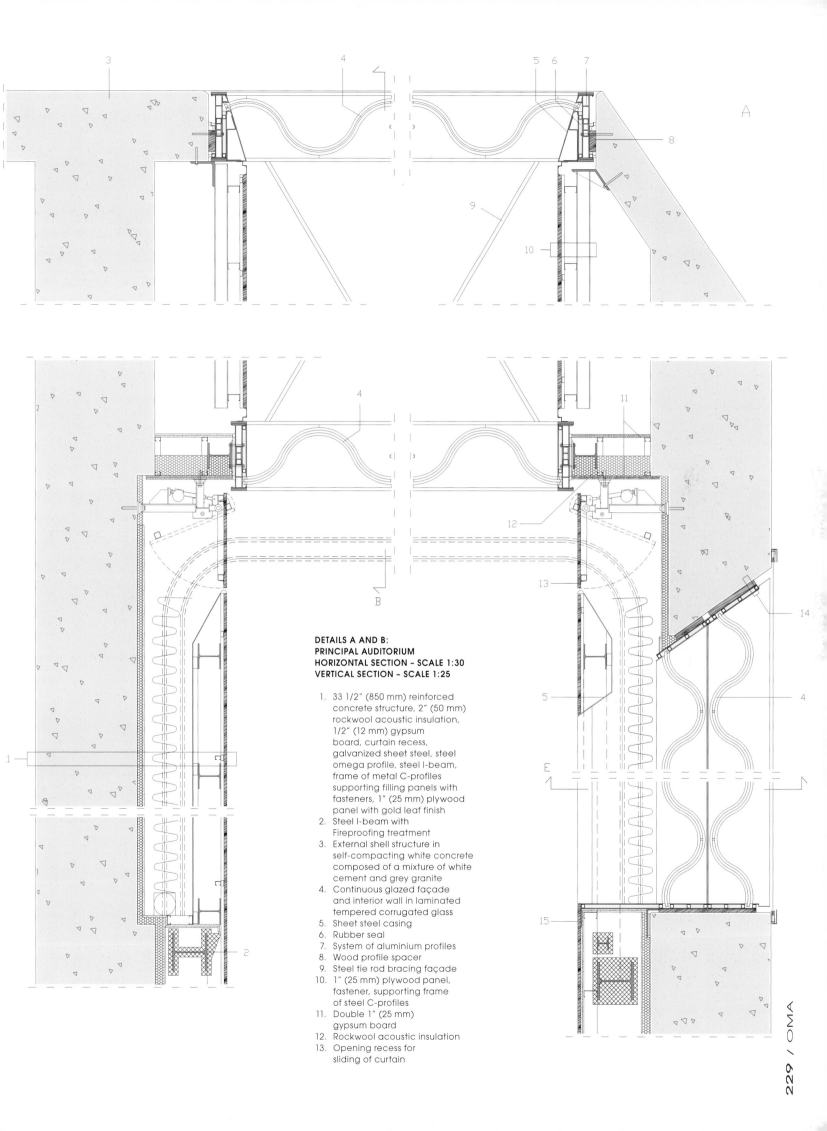

DETAILS A AND B:
PRINCIPAL AUDITORIUM
HORIZONTAL SECTION – SCALE 1:30
VERTICAL SECTION – SCALE 1:25

1. 33 1/2" (850 mm) reinforced concrete structure, 2" (50 mm) rockwool acoustic insulation, 1/2" (12 mm) gypsum board, curtain recess, galvanized sheet steel, steel omega profile, steel I-beam, frame of metal C-profiles supporting filling panels with fasteners, 1" (25 mm) plywood panel with gold leaf finish
2. Steel I-beam with Fireproofing treatment
3. External shell structure in self-compacting white concrete composed of a mixture of white cement and grey granite
4. Continuous glazed façade and interior wall in laminated tempered corrugated glass
5. Sheet steel casing
6. Rubber seal
7. System of aluminium profiles
8. Wood profile spacer
9. Steel tie rod bracing façade
10. 1" (25 mm) plywood panel, fastener, supporting frame of steel C-profiles
11. Double 1" (25 mm) gypsum board
12. Rockwool acoustic insulation
13. Opening recess for sliding of curtain

14. 1/4" (6 mm) sheet aluminium,
    frame of steel box-shaped
    profiles with rubber seal,
    1/4" (6 mm) sheet steel,
    wood spacer, reinforced
    concrete structure
15. Steel L-profile
16. Roof in 4" (100 mm)
    self-compacting white concrete,
    drainage layer, waterproofing
    membrane, triple layer of
    7 1/8" (180 mm) rock wool,
    vapour barrier, 15 3/4" (400 mm)
    reinforced concrete slab,
    3" (75 mm) acoustic
    board insulation, double

1" (25 mm) gypsum board
17. Double 1" (25 mm) gypsum
    board, 1 5/8" (40 mm) board
    insulation, acoustic insulation,
    composite steel I-beam with
    fireproofing treatment
18. Trussed structure formed
    by steel I- and L-beams
19. False ceiling in plywood
    panels on frame of steel profiles
20. Flooring on 2 3/4" (70 mm)
    screed with heating system,
    1 5/8" (40 mm) board insulation
    on height-adjustable joints,
    steel L-profile, 9 7/8" (250 mm)
    reinforced concrete slab

B

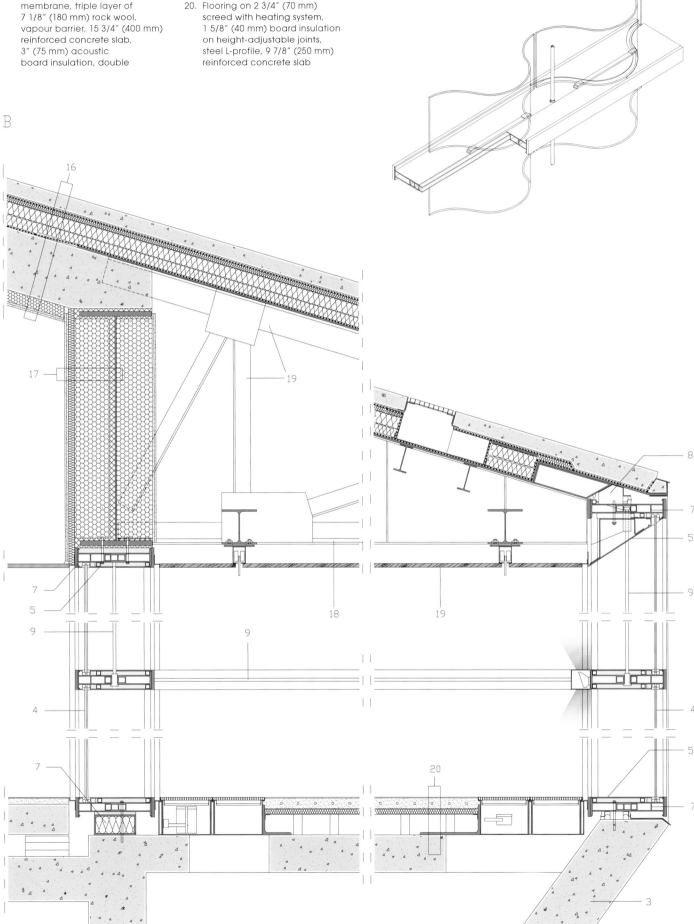

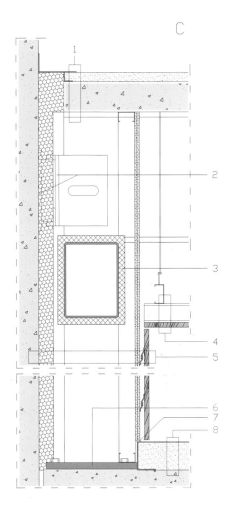

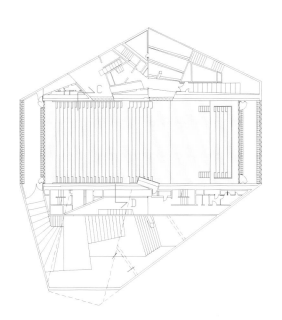

DETAILS C AND D:
PRINCIPAL AUDITORIUM
VERTICAL SECTIONS – SCALE 1:20

1. L-profile trim, 2" (50 mm) honed concrete floor, steel L-profile edging, 6 1/4" (160 mm) reinforced concrete slab, 27 1/8" (690 mm) steel I-beam (parallel to plane of section)
2. Connecting steel plates
3. 15 3/4 x 11 3/4" (400 x 300 mm) steel box beam with fireproofing treatment
4. False ceiling of 1" (25 mm) plywood panels with gold leaf finish, supporting frame of C-profiles on tie rods suspended from slab
5. 1" (25 mm) plywood panels with gold leaf finish, fastener, 1" (25 mm) double gypsum board, supporting frame of steel C-profiles, box-shaped profile upright (parallel to plane of section), air space, 3 1/8" (80 mm) acoustic board insulation, reinforced concrete structure
6. Steel plate support
7. Permanently elastic sealant
8. Floor on 5 3/4" (145 mm) screed, pre-cast reinforced concrete slab
9. Double continuous glazed façade in laminated tempered corrugated glass
10. Diffractal acoustic baffle, 1" (25 mm) double gypsum board, supporting frame of steel C-profiles, steel composite I-beam, acoustic board insulation, reinforced concrete structure
11. Frame of steel I-beams with fireproofing treatment
12. Reinforcing steel C-shaped profile with fireproofing treatment

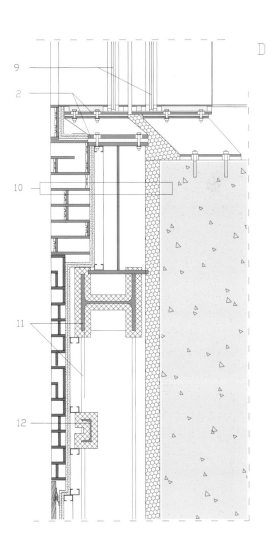

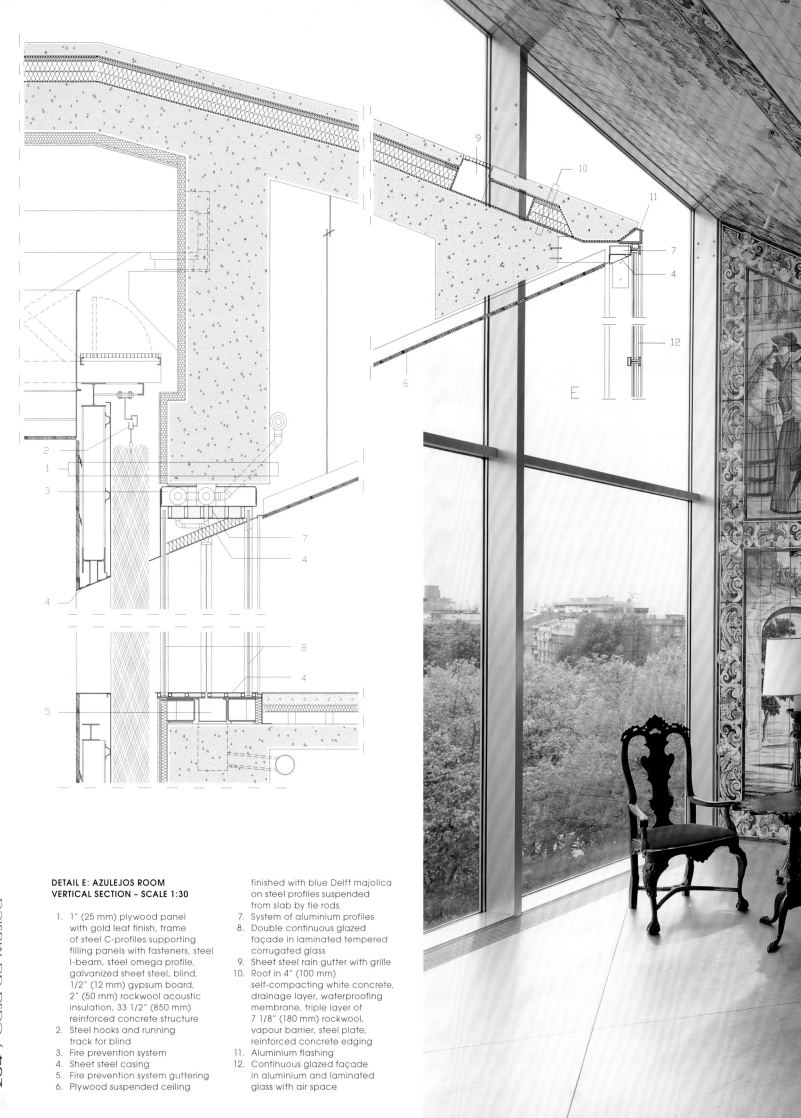

DETAIL E: AZULEJOS ROOM
VERTICAL SECTION – SCALE 1:30

1. 1" (25 mm) plywood panel with gold leaf finish, frame of steel C-profiles supporting filling panels with fasteners, steel I-beam, steel omega profile, galvanized sheet steel, blind, 1/2" (12 mm) gypsum board, 2" (50 mm) rockwool acoustic insulation, 33 1/2" (850 mm) reinforced concrete structure
2. Steel hooks and running track for blind
3. Fire prevention system
4. Sheet steel casing
5. Fire prevention system guttering
6. Plywood suspended ceiling

finished with blue Delft majolica on steel profiles suspended from slab by tie rods
7. System of aluminium profiles
8. Double continuous glazed façade in laminated tempered corrugated glass
9. Sheet steel rain gutter with grille
10. Roof in 4" (100 mm) self-compacting white concrete, drainage layer, waterproofing membrane, triple layer of 7 1/8" (180 mm) rockwool, vapour barrier, steel plate, reinforced concrete edging
11. Aluminium flashing
12. Continuous glazed façade in aluminium and laminated glass with air space

PROJECT CREDITS

VILLA NM – UPSTATE NEW YORK, USA
UN STUDIO / BEN VAN BERKEL

Location: Upstate New York / **Client:** Private / **Design:** 2000 / **Completion:** 2006 / **Gross Floor Area:** 2,691 ft^2 (250 m^2) / **Architect:** UN Studio / **Design Team:** Ben van Berkel with Olaf Gipser, Andrew Benn, Colette Parras, Jacco van Wengerden, Jan Debelius, Martin Kuitert / **Local Consultant:** Roemer Pierik / **Structural Consultant:** Robert Silman Associates / **Windows Framing:** Duratherm Window Corporation / **Flooring:** Bolidt / **Glass:** Pilkington

IXTAPA HOUSE – ZIHUATANEJO, MEXICO
LCM / FERNANDO ROMERO

Location: Punta Ixtapa, Zihuatanejo, Guerrero, Mexico / **Client:** Private / **Design:** 2001 / **Completion:** 2005 / **Gross Floor Area:** 14,531 ft^2 (1,350 m^2) / **Architect:** LCM/Fernando Romero / **Design Team:** Fernando Romero, Mark Seligson, Tatiana Bilbao, Juan Pablo Maza, Ernesto Gadea, Ivan Arellano, Martin Palardy, Aaron Hernández, Enrique Giner de los Ríos, Gonzalo Elizarrarás, Víctor Jaime, María Carrillo, David Téllez, Rodrigo Ramos / **Models:** Raul Vivar, Victor Jaime, Enrique Giner de los Ríos, Gonzalo Elizarrarás / **Site Manager:** René Cruz / **Structural Consultant:** Dys Ingenieria / **HVAC Consultant:** Diin Instalaciones / **Lighting:** Arquitectura Automática / **Services:** Inter Ingeniería y Construcciones

TWO HOUSES – PONTE DE LIMA, PORTUGAL
EDUARDO SOUTO DE MOURA

Location: Quinta de Anquião – Ponte de Lima, Portugal / **Client:** Miguel Cerquinho and Rui Branco / **Design:** 2001 / **Completion:** 2002 / **Architect:** Eduardo Souto de Moura / **Design Team:** Jorge Domingues, Joana Mira Corrêa, Ana Isabel, Joana Gaspar, Diogo Guimarães Adriana Miranda, Joaquim Portela / **Structural Consultant:** Lello & Associados / **Electrical Consultant:** Rodrigues Gomes & Associados / **Mechanical Consultant:** Ventarco / **General Contractors:** Coelho Construtores (Structures), Empalme – Sociedade de Construções (Finishes)

PRIVATE HOUSE – UDINE, ITALY
GRI E ZUCCHI ARCHITETTI ASSOCIATI

Location: Tarcento, Udine, Italy / **Client:** Private / **Design:** 2001 / **Completion:** 2004 / **Architect, Construction Manager:** Gri e Zucchi Architetti Associati / **Design Team:** Andrea Martinelli, Gianluca Buttolo, Alessandro Zuccolo, Tanja Ebersbach / **Structural Consultant:** Alessandro Nutta / **HVAC Consultant:** Alessandro Magrini / **Titanium Zinc Cladding:** Rheinzink

SUMMER HOUSE – ZAPALLAR, CHILE
ENRIQUE BROWNE & ARQUITECTOS ASOCIADOS

Location: Zapallar, Chile / **Client:** Private / **Design:** 1998 / **Completion:** 2001 / **Gross Floor Area:** 3,633 ft^2 (337.5 m^2) / **Architect:** Enrique Browne / **Design Team:** Andrés Frávega, Claudio Campos, Christine Filshill, Francisca Leighton / **Landscape Architect:** Juan Grimm, M. Angelica Schade / **Structural Consultant:** Vogel, Mujica y Breschi / **Contractor:** Juan Eduardo Saavedra / **Copper Contractor:** Procobre / **Glass Contractor:** Exxal

WELLENHAUS: HOUSE OF THE WAVES – HESSE, GERMANY
REICHEL ARCHITEKTEN

Location: Hesse, Germany / **Client:** Private / **Design:** 2001 / **Completion:** 2004 / **Gross Floor Area:** 20,742 ft^2 (1,927 m^2) / **Architect:** Alexander Reichel, Reichel Architekten / **Structural Consultant:** Pfeifer und Partner / **Landscape Architect:** Martin Altner / **Thermal Analysis, Mechanical Consultant:** Wagner und Klein / **Electrical Consultant:** Steinigeweg und Partner / **Lighting Equipments:** Belzner und Holmes / **Glass:** Tamfest / **Lifts:** Sieten Aufzuege Mainz / **Wall and Flooring:** Caparol / **Façade:** Frener & Reifer / **Technical details for this article:** courtesy Frener & Reifer

SPRINGTECTURE B – SHIGA, JAPAN
ENDO SHUHEI ARCHITECT INSTITUTE

Location: Biwa-ko, Shiga, Japan / **Client:** Private / **Design:** 2001 / **Completion:** 2002 / **Architect:** Endo Shuhei / **Gross Floor Area:** 2,196 ft² (204 m²)

CHESA FUTURA APARTMENTS – ST MORITZ, SWITZERLAND
FOSTER AND PARTNERS

Location: St Moritz, Switzerland / **Client:** SISA Immobilien / **Design:** 2000 / **Completion:** 2004 / **Architect:** Foster and Partners: Norman Foster, Graham Phillips, Stefan Behling, Matteo Fantoni, Sven Ollmann, Kate Carter, Jooryung Kim, Judit Kimpian, Tillman Lenz, Cristiana Paoletti, Stefan Robanus, Carolin Schaal, Horacio Schmidt, Thomas Spranger, Anna Sutor, Michele Tarroni, Huw Whitehead, Francis Aish / **Structural Consultant:** Edy Toscano, Ivo Diethelm, Arup / **Mechanical and Electrical Consultant:** EN/ES/TE, R & B Engineering / **Acoustic Consultant:** Edy Toscano **Cladding Consultant:** Emmer Pfenninger Partner / **Lighting Consultant:** Reflexion / **Concrete:** O Christoffel / **Timber Structure:** Holzbau Amann **Glass Lobbies:** Buehlmann / **Shingles:** Patrick Staeger / **Roof:** Dachtechnik / **Windows:** HFF Fenster und Fassaden / **Doors:** Lualdi / **Stone:** Vogt **Kitchens:** Bulthaup / **Timber Floors:** Hagetra / **Metalwork:** Pfister

COMMERCIAL AND RESIDENTIAL COMPLEX – BOHINJSKA BISTRICA, SLOVENIA
OFIS ARHITEKTI

Location: Bohinjska Bistrica, Slovenia / **Client:** Gradis G Group, Mercator / **Design:** 2006 / **Completion:** 2007 / **Architect:** Ofis Arhitekti / **Design Team:** Rok Oman, Špela Videcnik, Martina Lipicer, Meta Fortuna, Andrej Gregoric / **Structural Consultant:** Projecta / **Mechanical Consultant:** Bam-Bi / **Electrical Consultant:** EL-Projekt / **Traffic Consultant:** Tegainvest / **Main Contractor:** Gradis G Group / **Fibre Concrete Cladding:** Esal Anhovo / **Wood Cladding:** Mikek / **Windows:** Simer

MACALLEN RESIDENTIAL COMPLEX – BOSTON, USA
OFFICE dA

Location: Boston, USA / **Client:** Pappas Enterprises / **Design:** 2002 / **Completion:** 2007 / **Gross Floor Area:** 208,820 ft² (19,400 m²) / **Architect:** Office dA, Monica Ponce de Leon, Nader Tehrani / **Project Architect:** Dan Gallagher / **Project Manager:** Lisa Huang / **Design Team:** Ghazal Abassy, Remon Alberts, Hansy Luz Better, Scott Ewart, Katja Gischas, Anna Goodman, David Jeffries, Krists Karklins, Ethan Kushner, Christine Mueller, Julian Palacio, Penn Ruderman, Ahmad Reza Schricker, Harry Lowd / **Architect of Record:** Burt Hill / **Landscape Architect:** Landworks Studio / **Structural and Envelope Consultant:** Simpson Gumpertz & Heger / **MEP Consultant:** Commercial Construction Consulting / **Civil Engineering Consultant:** BSC Group **Acoustical Consultant:** Acentech / **Pool Consultant:** North East Aquatic Design / **Audio/Visual Consultant:** Audio Visual Designs **Geotechnical Consultant:** GEI Consultants / **Glass:** Viracon / **Window/Curtain Wall Systems:** Vistawall / **Aluminium Fins and Garage Screen:** Amstel / **Brick:** Endicott Clay Products / **Garden Roof:** American Hydrotech / **Exterior Metal Cladding/Composite Panels:** Alcoa

DOCUMENTATION AND INFORMATION CENTRE – BERGEN-BELSEN, GERMANY
ENGEL UND ZIMMERMANN ARCHITEKTEN

Location: Bergen-Belsen, Germany / **Client:** Lower Saxony Monument Foundation / **Design:** 2005 / **Completion:** 2007 / **Gross Floor Area:** 52,743 ft² (4,900 m²) / **Construction Costs:** 9 m Euros / **Architect:** KSP Engel und Zimmermann Architekten / **Design Team:** Henner Winkelmüller, Konstanze Beelitz / **Project Management:** Ulrich Gremmelspacher, Michael Reiff / **Renderings:** Atelier Berthold Weidner / **Landscape Architect:** Sinai **Electrical Consultant:** Ingenieurbüro Lindhorst IBL / **Acoustical Consultant:** Müller-BBM / **Structural Consultant:** Wetzel & von Seht / **Light Planning Consultant:** Toworx / **Air Conditioning Consultant:** NEK Ingenieurgruppe / **Exhibition Planning:** Hans Dieter Schaal / **Construction Management:** Hermann Timpe, Michael Brinkmann, Bernd Habersaat / **Contractor:** Wallbrecht Bauunternehmung / **Electrical Services:** Heinken Elektrotechnik **Exhibition:** Hypsos / **Glass Façade:** Wagener / **Flooring:** Jeschke / Freese / **Technical Furnishing and Lighting:** MCI Studio

MEISO NO MORI MUNICIPAL FUNERAL HALL – KAKAMIGAHARA, JAPAN
TOYO ITO & ASSOCIATES

Location: Kakamigahara, Gifu, Japan / **Client:** Kakamigahara City / **Design:** 2004 / **Completion:** 2006 / **Gross Floor Area:** 24,434 ft^2 (2,270 m^2) / **Architect:** Toyo Ito & Associates, Architects / **Structural Consultant:** Sasaki Structural Consultants / **Mechanical Consultant:** Kankyo Engineering / **Landscape Architect:** Professor Mikiko Ishikawa, Keio University / **Lighting Consultant:** Lightdesign / **General Contractor:** Joint Venture of Toda, Ichikawa, Tenryu

CUBE TOWER – GUADALAJARA, MEXICO
ESTUDIO CARME PINÓS

Location: Puerta de Hierro, Guadalajara, Mexico / **Client:** Cube Internacional / **Design:** 2002 / **Completion:** 2005 / **Gross Floor Area:** 75,347 ft^2 (7,000 m^2) / **Architect:** Estudio Carme Pinós / **Project Architects:** Juan Antonio Andreu, Samuel Arriola, Frederic Jordan, Cesar Vergés **Design Team:** Agustín Pérez-Torres, Holger Hennefarth, Caroline Lambrechts / **Structural Consultant:** Luis Bozzo / **Contractor:** Anteus Constructora **Wooden Façade:** Stellac Wood Mikkeli Oy / **Glass:** Saint-Gobain / **Concrete:** Cemex / **Lifts:** Otis / **Automation:** Alta Tecnologia en Instalaciones **Internal Wood Panels:** Prodema

METZO COLLEGE – DOETINCHEM, THE NETHERLANDS
ERICK VAN EGERAAT ASSOCIATED ARCHITECTS

Location: Doetinchem, The Netherlands / **Client:** Stichting CoVoa, Doetinchem / **Design:** 2002 / **Completion:** 2006 / **Gross Floor Area:** 176,528 ft^2 (16,400 m^2) / **Architects:** Erick van Egeraat, Michiel Raaphorst / **Design Team:** Rowan van Wely, Ann-Christin Hillebrand, Paul Blonk, Marie Prunault, Tanya Albertoe, Marlies Quack, Ronald Ubels, Suzanne Lüthi, Gertjan Nijhoff, Léon Wielaard, Ard Hoksbergen, Peter Toering, Ellen van Genechten **Renderings:** Peter Heavens, Steven Simons / **Structural Consultant:** ABT-C / **Façade Consultant:** Alkondor / **Electrical and Mechanical Consultant:** ABT-I / **Acoustical Consultant:** Peutz / **Landscape Architect:** Poldergast / **General Contractor:** Schutte Bouwbedrijf / **Mechanical Services:** W.A. Kemkens / **Electrical Services:** Unica Installatietechniek / **Flooring:** Unipro / **Polyester Concrete Panels:** Polyproducts / **Gym Facilities:** Janssen-Fritsen / **Lockers and Counters:** Varwijk Interieurbouwers / **Window Frames, Glazed Façade:** Schüco

SHIPPING AND TRANSPORT COLLEGE – ROTTERDAM, THE NETHERLANDS
NEUTELINGS & RIEDIJK

Location: Lloyd Pier, Rotterdam, The Netherlands / **Client:** Stichting Scheepvaart en Transportonderwijs Rotterdam / **Design:** 2000 / **Completion:** 2005 / **Gross Floor Area:** 322,917 ft^2 (30,000 m^2) / **Construction Costs:** 42 m Euros / **Architect:** Neutelings Riedijk Architecten / **Design Team:** Willem Jan Neutelings, Michiel Riedijk,Sven Verbruggen, Jago van Bergen, Wessel Vreugdenhill Kenichi Teramoto, Elisabeth Eriksen, Sandra Schuster, Dimitri Meessen, Helena Casanova / **Structural and HVAC Consultant:** ABT / **Physics Consultant:** Peutz & Associés Molenhoek / **Contractor:** Heijmans IBC Bouw, Amsterdam Schiphol / **Artwork:** Peter Breevoort

GALWAY-MAYO INSTITUTE OF TECHNOLOGY – GALWAY, IRELAND
MURRAY O'LAOIRE ARCHITECTS

Location: Galway, Ireland / **Client:** Galway-Mayo Institute of Technology / **Design:** 1998 / **Completion:** 2003 / **Gross Floor Area:** 110,481 ft^2 (10,264 m^2) / **Construction Costs:** 20 m Euros / **Architect:** Murray O'Laoire Architects / **Structural Consultant:** O'Connor Sutton Cronin **Mechanical & Electrical Consultant:** Varming Mulcahy Reilly Associates / **Façade Consultant:** Arup Façade Engineers / **Landscape Architect:** Murray O'Laoire Architects / **Contractor:** JJ Rhatigan & Co / **Sails Prepatinated Copper Cladding:** KME – Tecu Patina

SIMMONS HALL, MIT – CAMBRIDGE, USA
STEVEN HOLL ARCHITECTS

Location: Cambridge, Massachusetts, USA / **Client:** Massachusetts Institute of Technology / **Design:** 1999 / **Completion:** 2002 / **Senior Project Manager:** Jonathan Himmel / **Project Manager:** Thomas Murray, Casali Group / **Design Architects:** Steven Holl, Timothy Bade / **Project Architect:** Timothy Bade / **Assistant Project Architects:** Ziad Jamaleddine, Anderson Lee / **Project Team:** Peter Burns, Gabriela Barman-Kramer, Makram elKadi, Annette Goderbauer, Mimi Hoang, Ziad Jameleddine, Matt Johnson, Erik Langdalen, Anderson Lee, Ron-Hui Lin / **Local Architect:** Perry Dean Rogers and Partners / **Structural Consultant:** Guy Nordenson & Associates / **Mechanical Consultant:** Ove Arup & Partners / **Lighting Consultant:** Fisher Marantz Stone / **Contractor:** Daniel O'Connell's Sons / **Precast Concrete:** Beton Bolduc / **Cast-in-Place Concrete:** S&F Concrete Corporation / **Concrete Supplier:** Aggregate Industries / **Rebar:** Harris Rebar / **Rebar Installer:** Bartlund / **Cladding & Windows:** Cheviot

RICHARD E. LINDNER ATHLETICS CENTER – UNIVERSITY OF CINCINNATI, USA
BERNARD TSCHUMI ARCHITECTS

Location: Cincinnati, Ohio, USA / **Client:** University of Cincinnati / **Design:** 2001 / **Completion:** 2006 / **Gross Floor Area:** 254,028 ft^2 (23,600 m^2) **Construction Costs:** 53 m USD / **Architect:** Bernard Tschumi Architects / **Design Team:** Bernard Tschumi, Kim Starr, Phu Hoang, Robert Holton, Jane Kim, Nicolas Martin, Eva Sopeoglou, Joel Aviles, Chong-zi Chen, Irene Cheng, Jonathan Chace, Adam Dayem, William Feuerman, Thomas Goodwill, Daniel Holguin, Matthew Hufft, Michaela Metcalf, Valentin Bontjes van Beek, Allis Chee, Justin Moore / **Local Architect:** Glaserworks **Construction Manager:** Turner Construction Company / **Structural Consultant:** THP, Arup / **Mechanical and Electrical Consultant:** Heapy Engineers, Arup / **Landscape Architect:** Human Nature / **Master Plan Consultant:** Hargreaves Associates / **Audio Visual Consultant:** ICB Audio & Video Equipment / **Interior Design:** Design Details / **Museum Graphics:** Eva Maddox Branded Environments / **General Contractor:** Dick Corporation / **Steel Contractor:** Steel Services Corporation / **Mechanical Contractor:** Rfc Mechanical / **Electrical Contractor:** EBI / **Windows:** Waltek / **Precast Concrete:** High Concrete Technology / **Curtain Wall:** Geiger Construction Products / **Flooring:** AIC Contracting / **Ceramic and Terrazzo:** Axis Interior Systems / **Framing:** Cleveland Construction / **Masonry:** Cost Company / **Concrete:** Baker Concrete Construction

CAMPUS RECREATION CENTER – UNIVERSITY OF CINCINNATI, USA
MORPHOSIS / THOM MAYNE

Location: Cincinnati, Ohio, USA / **Client:** University of Cincinnati / **Design:** 1999 / **Completion:** 2006 / **Gross Floor Area:** 376,737 ft^2 (35,000 m^2) **Construction Costs:** 74 m USD / **Architect:** Morphosis, Thom Mayne / **Design Team:** Thom Mayne, Kim Groves, Kristina Loock, Ben Damron, Henriette Bier, Marty Doscher, Ted Kane, Silvia Kuhle, Eric Nulman, Martin Summers, Brandon Welling, Jason Anthony, Crister Cantrell, Manish Dessai, Hanjo Gellink, Lisa Hseih, Dwoyne Keith, Patricia Schneider, Scott Severson, Paxton Sheldahl, John Skillern, Christian Taubert, Petar Vrcibradic, Eui Sung Yi, Natalia Traverso / **Local Architect:** KZF Design / **Structural Concept:** Ove Arup and Partners / **Structural Consultant:** THP / **Mechanical, Electrical, Plumbing Consultant:** Heapy Engineering / **Landscape Architect:** Hargreaves Associates / **Interior Design:** Morphosis / **Graphic Artist:** Rebeca Mendez / **Muralists:** Painted Surfaces, James Griffith and Susanna Dadd / **General Contractor:** Turner Construction / **Steel Contractor:** Sofco Erectors / **Construction Manager:** Messer/Jacobs, a joint venture / **Metal/Glass Curtain Wall:** Waltek / **Precast Concrete:** Concrete Technology / **Metal Roofing:** Bemo/USA / **Glass:** Viracon / **Interior Finishes:** USG / **Walls/Flooring:** Eternit/ Swisspear / **Ceramic Wall and Floor Tile in Pool Area:** Dal-Tile, American Olean / **Carpet Manufacturer:** Interface / **Furnishings:** Knoll / **Chairs:** Vitra / **Cladding:** Reynobond, Alcoa

CASA DA MÚSICA – PORTO, PORTUGAL
OMA / REM KOOLHAAS

Project: Casa da Música, Porto, Portugal / **Client:** The City of Porto / **Design:** 2001 / **Completion:** 2005 / **Gross Floor Area:** 236,806 ft^2 (22,000 m^2) **Architects:** OMA, Rem Koolhaas and Ellen van Loon / **Project Architects:** Adrianne Fisher, Michelle Howard / **Design Team:** Fernando Romero Havaux, Isabel da Silva, Nuno Rosado, Robert Choeff, Barbara Wolff, Saskia Simon, Christian von der Muelde, Rita Armando, Philip Koenen, Peter Mueller, Krystian Keck, Eduarda Lima, Christoff Scholl, Alex de Jong, Alois Zierl, Uwe Herlijn, Olaf Hitz, Jorge Toscano, Duarte Santos, Nelson Carvalho, Stefanie Wandinger / **Interior Curtains and Auditorium Design:** Petra Blaisse / Inside Outside / **Local Architect:** ANC Architects, Jorge Carvalho **Structural and HVAC Consultant:** Arup London / **Façade Consultant:** van Santen/Arup Facades / **Fire Consultant:** Ohm/Gerisco / **Acoustics Consultant:** Dorseer Blesgraaf / **Scenography:** Ducks Scéno / **Auditorium Seating:** Maarten van Severen / **Furniture:** Atelier Daciano da Costa

About THE PLAN

THE PLAN is one of the most acclaimed architectural and design reviews on the Italian market and, thanks to its strong international approach, is among the most widely distributed and read magazines world-wide. THE PLAN's editorial philosophy is to provide in-depth understanding of architecture presenting key projects as information and learning tools, which are highly profitable for the professionals who read the magazine. Content quality is a prerequisite. Each project is prepared with the utmost attention, from the construction details through to images and graphic design.

www.theplan.it

THE PLAN Staff

Editor-in-Chief: NICOLA LEONARDI
Art Director: CARLOTTA ZUCCHINI
Managing Editor: ADRIANA DALL'OCCA DELL'ORSO
Creative Director: RICCARDO PIETRANTONIO
Graphic & Editing: GIANFRANCO CESARI, GIANLUCA RAIMONDO
Editorial Staff: LAURA COCURULLO, FEDERICO MASTRORILLI, ILARIA MAZZANTI, SILVIA MONTI, ALICE POLI
General Manager: GUGLIELMO BOZZI BONI
Administration: SERENA PRETI

First published in the United Kingdom in 2009 by
Thames & Hudson Ltd, 181A High Holborn, London WC1V 7QX

www.thamesandhudson.com

First published in 2009 in hardcover in the United States of America by
Thames & Hudson Inc., 500 Fifth Avenue, New York, New York 10110

thamesandhudsonusa.com

© 2009 The Plan editions, Cube srl, Bologna
This edition © 2009 Thames & Hudson Ltd, London
Photographs © 2009 The photographers

British Library Cataloguing-in-Publication Data
A catalogue record for this book is available from the British Library

Library of Congress Catalog Card Number 2008911518

ISBN: 978-0-500-34253-4

Printed and bound in Italy

Picture Credits

Villa NM (012-021) © Christian Richters, Courtesy UN Studio
Ixtapa House (022-026 / 028-031) © Luis Gordoa,
(027) © Michael Calderwood
Two Houses (032-043) © Bill Timmerman
Private House (044-053) © Andrea Pertoldeo
Summer House (054-063) © Guy Wenborne and Enrique Browne
Wellenhaus (064-073) © Christian Richters, Courtesy Frener & Reifer
Springtecture B (074-075) © Toshiharu Kitajima, **(076/079)** © Yoshiharu Matsumura, **(078/081)** © Toshiharu Kitajima
Chesa Futura (082-093) © Nigel Young / Foster & Partners
Commercial and Residential Complex (094-103) © Tomaž Gregoric
Macallen Residential Complex (104-113) © John Horner
Documentation and Information Centre (114-121) © Klemens Ortmeyer/fabpics
Meiso no Mori Municipal Funeral Hall (122-123/128) © JA Company SHINKENCHIKU, **(124/126/127)** © Toyo Ito & Associates, Architects
Cube Tower (130-145) © Duccio Malagamba
Metzo College (146-157) © Christian Richters
Shipping and Transport College (158-171) © Jeroen Musch
Galway-Mayo Institute of Technology (172-179) © Ross Kavanagh
Simmons Hall (180-191) © Andy Ryan, Courtesy MIT Department of Facilities
Richard E. Lindner Athletics Center (192-201) © Peter Mauss – Esto
Campus Recreation Center (202-216) © Roland Halbe
Casa da Música (216-235) © Christian Richters

Text Credits

Villa NM by Emiliano Gandolfi
Two Houses by Francesco Pagliari
A Private House by Francesco Pagliari
Summer House by Enrique Browne
Macallen Residential Complex by Raymund Ryan
Meiso no Mori Municipal Funeral Hall by Lorena Alessio
Cube Tower by Francesco Pagliari
Shipping and Transport College by Emiliano Gandolfi
Casa da Música by Lucy Bullivant

All the original drawings in this volume
have been elaborated by The Plan Editions